clear GLASS

Creating New Perspectives

Imprint
The Deutsche Bibliothek is registering this publication in the
Deutsche Nationalbibliographie; detailed bibliographical infor-
mation can be found on the internet at http://dnb.ddb.de

ISBN 978-3-03768-003-2

© 2009 by Braun Publishing AG
www.braun-publishing.ch

1st edition 2009

Editorial staff:
Sophie Steybe, Natascha Saupe
Draft texts by the architects. Text editing: Chris van Uffelen
Translation:
Alice Bayandin
Graphic concept:
Michaela Prinz
Layout:
Natascha Saupe

Chris van Uffelen

clear
GLASS
Creating New Perspectives

BRAUN

Immaterial material

Glass is possibly the most important building material of all. Windows are found in practically every house and, with the exception of a few special forms of window fillings (transenna, alabaster), all of them are sealed using glass. Without glass, the wish to illuminate the interior while protecting it from harsh climate would be an impossible task. Even though the isolating properties of glass may still be improved upon, it is also used in warmer regions as a climate barrier that provides a transparent but definitive periphery for inhabitable space. It wasn't always like this. The region where glass originated, eastern Mediterranean, has such a mild climate, that the need to cover windows did not exist. For this reason, glass does not even appear in architecture in the first 2000 years of its 4000 year history. At the beginning, glass was used primarily for jewelry and vessels, and the techniques for working with it improved gradually, culminating in the discovery of glass blowing which produces thin glass, eventually leading to the production of glass that is ideal for windows. But cast glass predominated at first, and fragments of 12 millimeters thick slabs which were used to build glasshouses have been unearthed in Pompeii. Roman glass originally reached sizes of 70 by 100 centimeters. As the material spread around Europe with the Roman expansion in 1st century A.D., the word glass presumably developed from the Germanic glesum (shining, transparent). However, throughout the Early Middle Ages glass remained expensive, and the first private homes sealed with glass appeared only at the end of the 12th century in England. In other regions homes were haunted by drafts throughout the Middle Age. The first age of glass was the Gothic period, when architecture became divided into a load-bearing structure and the glass that used to fill it out. Glass surfaces of churches grew in size, culminating in 1248 in the impressive clerestory windows of the Beauvais Cathedral, which outlined the building's form, expanding like a sail. Whereas windows were mostly red and blue during the High Gothic period, clear class and Grisaille painting were preferred in the Late Gothic.

Large glass surfaces were common in Northern European Renaissance (Robet Smythson's "Hardwick Hall – more glass than wall" 1590–97). Individual panes became significantly larger and more regular than in the Gothic. Glass became readily available between the 16th and 19th centuries. This development was sped by the demand for orangeries in French gardens built during the Baroque period.

These protective pavilions were used to entertain guests in the summer months, which encouraged their shift from the garden periphery to the most prominent position in the center. Around 1700, cast glass was available in France in nearly every size. Clear glass was especially needed for mirrors, like those in the Hall of Mirrors in Versailles. Horse carriages needed especially resistant glass, which led to improvements in glass manufacture. Glass houses came into fashion after English gardens replaced the French in prominence.

Joseph Paxton's Crystal Palace built for the 1851 World Exhibition in London was impressive, if not very appropriate as a representational building, being a completely glazed structure supported by a cast iron frame with wrought iron and wood elements.

The chemical process of glassmaking remained largely unchanged during its 3900-year history: quartz sand, a ubiquitously available raw material, is molten at approximately 1500 degrees Celsius and gradually cooled under controlled conditions. The exact chemical composition of glass was not determined until around 1900. Glass consists primarily of silica (SiO_2 72.5%), sodium carbonate (Na_2O 13.4%) and calcium oxide (CaO 8.9%), as well as traces of magnesium and aluminum, iron and manganese oxides. This discovery enabled the mixture to be controlled with more precision, and soon it was believed that glass would become the perfect universal building material. In its original, 'intuitive' composition glass is hard, able to bear loads in its block form and remains chemically passive, making it resistant to acids. Its brittle nature was the last barrier that had to be overcome. This inspired the writer Paul Scheerbart to envision a utopian glass architecture which would improve not only buildings, but also society and human spirit itself. Bruno Taut's Glass Pavilion erected at the 1914 Werkbund (German Work Federation) Exhibition in Cologne realized this expressionist utopian vision. A domed structure of clear and stained plate and cast glass contained only a modern interpretation of a baroque staircase and a fountain: glass pour le glass. The material's significance for Classic Modernism can also be gathered in Ludwig Mies van der Rohe's legendary glass skyscraper designs. ✗

Glass walls, such as the famous curtain wall on the Bauhaus building in Dessau, were made possible thanks to safety glass which had been developed already in the 1870s. New load-bearing frames enabled construction of ribbon glazing and glazed corners free of all support function, as exemplified by Gerrit Rietveld's Utrecht Rietveld Schröder House.

Modern manufacturing methods, like conveyor belt plate glass manufacture by Ford, made glass cheap and available in all forms. Unfortunately, many of the rounded plates from the 19th century have been replaced by flat ones in the course of restoration. This age has also produced metaphorical use of glass in architecture that remains a favorite to this day. In describing his design for the League of Nations building in Geneva, Hannes Meyer said, "instead of elbowing corridors for diplomats' zigzags, open glazed spaces for public negotiations between open people". Glass continued to be used in this tradition after the Second World War in Post-war and Late Modernism.

Philip Johnson (House in Connecticut, 1949) and Mies ✗ van der Rohe (Farnsworth House, 1946–51) built houses completely out of glass, whose transparency could be outdone only in the course of the last decade (Werner Sobek Haus R 128, 1997–2001). The Lever House by SOM (1951–52) makes use of green heat-absorbing glass while Mies van der Rohe's Seagram Building (1954–58) utilizes bronze-toned glass to match its frame. Glass staining, however, taxed the buildings' light and air conditioning efficiency, which Le Corbusier had already attempted to create with his Cité refugee in Paris, but Richard Rogers finally succeeded in doing with his Lloyd's Building (1979–84). It is around this time that glass began being used as part of the building's frame, as in House Benthem (Benthem Crouwel, 1983–84), with structural reinforcement made of glass.

Modern pre-stressed glass is five times more stable than normal window panes and is capable of taking on structural roles to the extent that probably Scheerbart himself couldn't imagine. But the function of modern glass does not end here: solar elements can be embedded in it; it can be screen printed, laminated or coated in order to give it various functions. Even it's most inherent property, translucency, can be altered at the touch of a button by applying an electric current to an embedded layer of liquid crystals (Rem Koolhaas (OMA) Prada Store, New York 2001).

Chris van Uffelen

IMMATERIAL

Villamoda, 2001
Address: Kuwait Free Trade Zone – Shuwaikh,
Shaniya, Kuwait. **Client:** Majed Al Sabah. **Gross floor
area:** 8,000 m². **Materials:** glass, concrete, stone, steel.

Vogue as a mirage

ARCHITECTS: Pierfrancesco Cravel /
pfcarchitects

Built on an unused dock area, the fashion mall is arranged like a bazaar. Divided into ten stand alone
brand-specific areas for high end luxury retailers and
two multi-brand shops, the overarching design unites
the common areas. Slender columns and large screens
of glass create a wide and high space, concealing its
boarders at first glance. The stores' individual style
guides go into effect only behind the glass separators
that define their area.

04

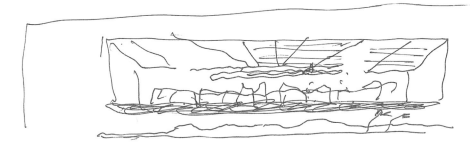

05

06

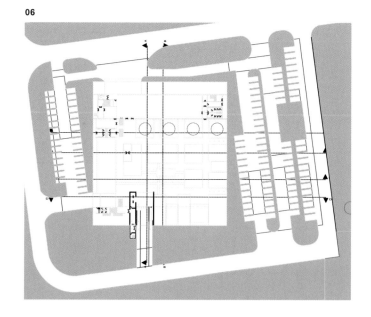

Mediatheek Delft, 2007
Address: Vesteplein 100, Delft, The Netherlands.
Client: City of Delft, The Netherlands. **Gross floor area:** 9,940 m². **Materials:** glass, steel, brick, ceramic elements, hardstone.

Old-to-new ceiling

ARCHITECTS: Liesbeth van der Pol /
Dok architecten, Aat Vos / AEQUO Architects

The renewal of the Mediatheek is characterized by color and light as well as a contrast between contemporary and traditional materials, which results in various atmospheres. This, in turn, creates an inextricable unity, fitting in with historical architecture in Delft. Traditional orange-colored brick and dark boarding have been used, and together with hardstone details, they make for a classic urban look. In each department, color and organizing elements produce distinction and identification. At the entrance, a glass construction with a ten meter height is placed as an extreme "welcoming gesture". A light well created using a void and a striking glass roof covering the breadth of the building has been added. Light is given great depth and led into the very heart of the building, letting its interior be understood with just one glance.

03

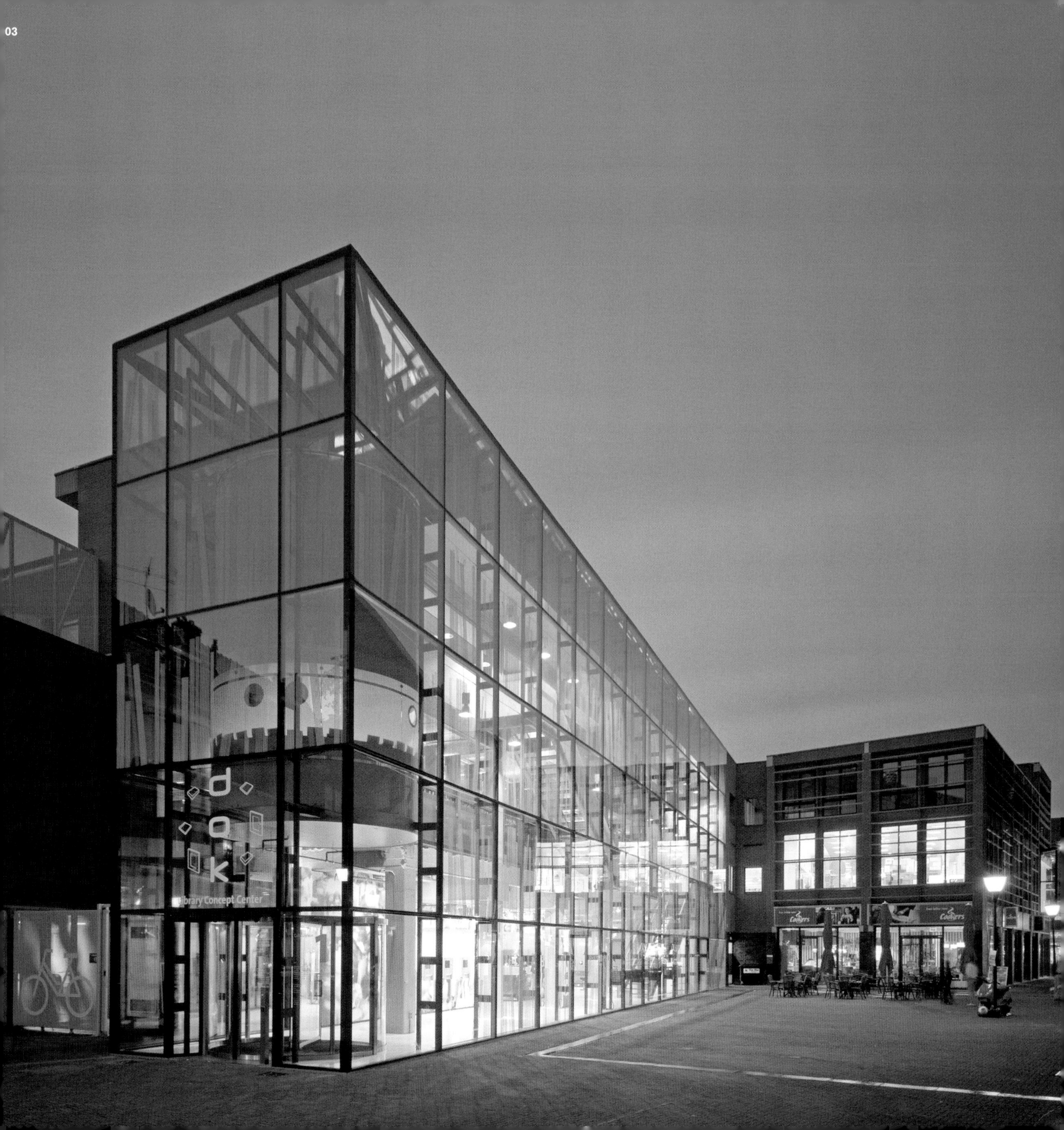

04

05

06

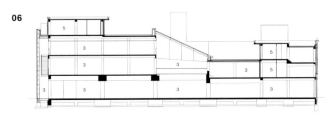

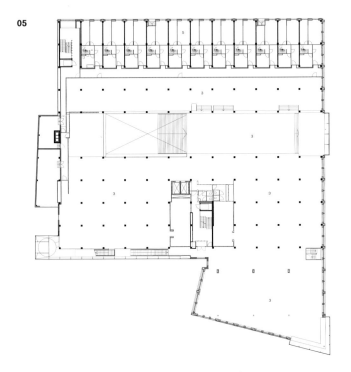

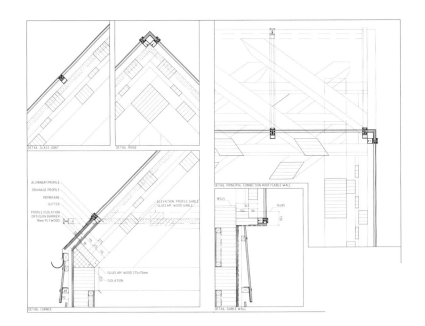

01

Tautra Maria Convent, 2006
Address: Tautra, Frosta, Norway. **Client:** Cisterian Nuns, Tautra Convent. **Gross floor area:** 2,000 m².
Materials: wood, glass, steel, concrete, slate stones.

Thanking Blessed Mary for light Divine

ARCHITECTS: Jensen & Skodvin Architects

This project is a new monastery for 18 nuns, complete with a small church and all facilities needed for a sustainable living. The original program was reduced by ca. 30% by eliminating almost all corridors in the project. This was made possible by analyzing the way the monastery works. Usually, when all the nuns are assembled, they gather in one of the four main rooms, which can therefore also act as "corridors" and traffic areas. Most of the rooms are unique and have very different requirements. This stated a need for architectural flexibility as well as adequate daylight reaching each of the rooms located within the horizontal layout. For this reason, the project consists of a system of spaces connected to each other at the corners using courts.

02

01 Roof construction **02** Façade detail **03** Front view **04** Interior chapel

Heimbs Coffeeroaster flagship store, 2007
Address: Bohlweg / Damm Schlossarkaden Braunschweig, Germany. **Glass engineers:** OKALUX GmbH. **Structural engineers:** Drewes + Speth. **Light planning:** Fahlke & Dettmer Licht in der Architektur. **Client:** Heimbs Kaffee GmbH & Co. KG. **Gross floor area:** 183 m². **Materials:** coffee beans on a bed of silicone inside insulated glass OKA X.

A glass of coffee
ARCHITECTS: Despang Architekten

Heimbs, who have been in the coffee roasting business for over 125 years, present themselves to the awaiting public for the first time in the Braunschweiger Castle, which has been recently reopened as a mall. In contrast to the representation of coffee that has been mediated by pop culture and post modernism, here the bean is presented in an opulent mantle and in its fullness. The counters and the space itself are transformed into coffee chutes and the guest is surrounded by the origins of the drink's flavor as it enjoys the product. To simulate the process of roasting using red/orange/yellow light, OKALUX, the world market leader in custom insulated glass paneling developed a unique solution, whereby the beans were placed inside a bed of white silicon.

04

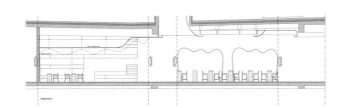

05

06

Waldhaus Flims Mountain Resort & Spa, 2004
Address: Waldhaus Flims Mountain Resort & Spa,
Flims Waldhaus, Switzerland. **Client:** Waldhaus Flims
Mountain Resort & Spa AG. **Materials:** glass, oak,
cherrywood, grey quartzite.

Floating through centuries

ARCHITECTS: Architektur & Designbüro Pia M.
Schmid, Hans Peter Fontana / Fontana & Partner

Edging over the old quarry stone wall surrounding a former tennis court, the floating lantern project is located
on the site of an old swimming pool, which has been
moved to a restored Jugendstil pavilion. The lantern's
glass façade reflects the forest, the sky, the mountains
and the silhouette of the pavilion's Jugendstil façade.
Thus, the old and the new melt into each other. Sophisticated illumination technology located inside the
floor of the inner pool transforms the glass cube even
in nighttime with its ever-changing interplay of color to
a landmark attraction – a true magic lantern.

04

05

06

07

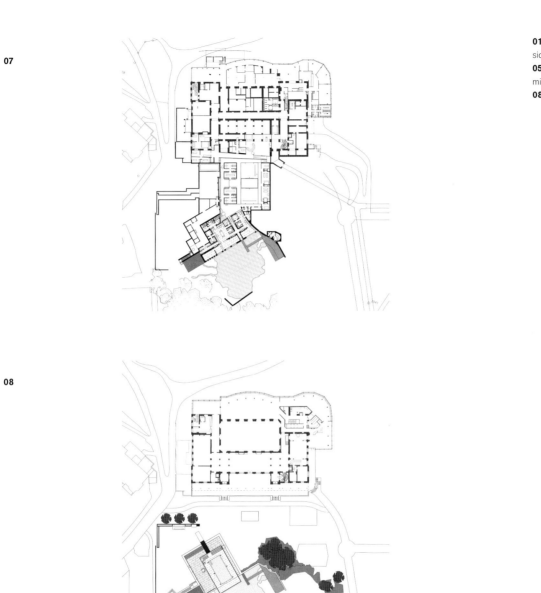

08

09

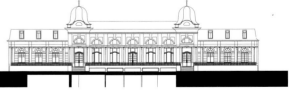

27

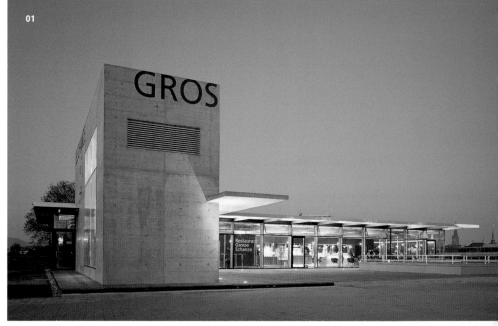

01

Elevator system Grosse Schanze, 2008
Address: Main station Berne, Switzerland. **Color consultant restaurant:** Kontur2. **Client:** GSAG Grosse Schanze AG. **Gross floor area:** 400 m². **Materials:** glass, concrete, metal.

Rapture of the tube
ARCHITECTS: GWJARCHITEKTEN

The elevator system connects Berne's train station to the university campus and the Länggass quarter above. With the new design and increase of capacity, a new world of sensory experience is created at the connecting station between the old city and the Grosser Schanze. The completely hollowed-out shaft leads daylight through six floors down to the platform underpass. The suspended steel staircase acts as an accompanying installation and a viewable climbing scaffolding. Three transparent elevator cabins convey the experience of dynamic movement and transform the formerly featureless urban location into a vertical space with three adventure-filled tubes. The elevator tower with a large window on the movable elevator mechanism acts as a landmark and a reference point on the university grounds.

02

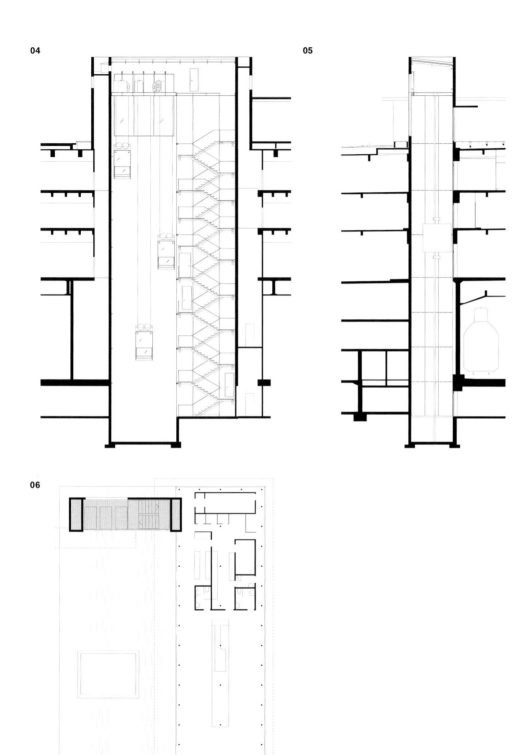

04

05

06

HA·LO headquarters, 2000
Address: 5980 W Touhy Ave, Niles, Illinois, USA.
Client: CenterPoint Properties. **Gross floor area:**
24,835 m². **Materials:** glass, steel.

HA-LLOw glass

ARCHITECTS: Murphy / Jahn

The conceptual ideas about the HA·LO headquarters deal with urban planning, function and technology. The building is arranged like a simple and clear diagram with maximum transparency. Traditionally, light has been directed at the material fabric of a building, illuminating the solid, while here light is the essence of the design. The building is luminous, not illuminated, moderating the natural and the artificial light. The functions are placed around a seven-story open court. The low floors are loft-type offices. The top two floors are showrooms and executive offices around a two-story sky court. This clear stacking is readable at the entry facade and contributes to the building's transparency.

04

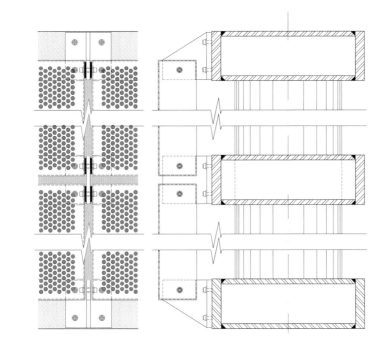

01 The transparent glass façade of the HA•LO building is supported by glass mullions **02** Interior view **03** Exterior view **04** Section **05** Section **06** Glass detail **07** Glass elevator

05

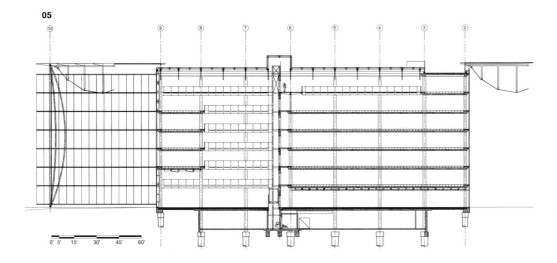

0' 5' 15'   30'   45'   60'

Renovation WY building, 2007
Address: High Tech Campus 37, Eindhoven, The Netherlands. **Design team:** Inbo/JHK samenwerkende architecten, Juurlink [+] Geluk. **Client:** Philips Electronics Nederland bv. **Gross floor area:** 25,500 m². **Materials:** glass, steel, natural stone.

Very welcome

ARCHITECTS: JHK Architecten

The new entryway, part of a complete renovation of the building WY, is designed as a slender and transparent volume in contrast to the heavy office building itself. The building WY dates from 1968 and has been one of the scene-setting laboratory buildings on the High Tech Campus in Eindhoven. It has recently undergone a complete renovation. The out-of-date laboratories have been transformed into light, transparent offices and test spaces, and a new entry hall volume was added. The use of steel and glass in the entry hall construction refers to the high-tech character of the campus, whereas the walls, built out of natural stone, refer to the architecture of the sixties, which used to be omnipresent here. The renovation of the building reveals an interesting three-way dialogue between rough stone, refined steel and glass.

04

01 Entrance area **02** Front view **03** Building with entrance **04** Sketch **05** Entrance section **06** Entrance ground floor plan **07** Stairway inside the entrance area

05

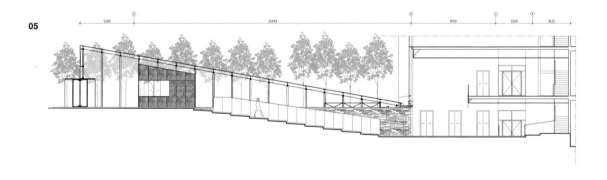

06

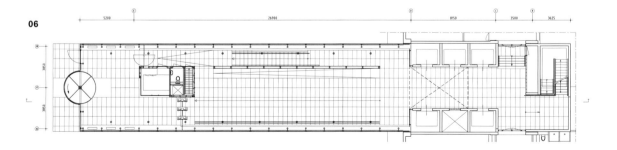

TV Asahi, 2003
Address: 6-9-1 Roppongi, Minato-ku Tokyo, Japan.
Structural engineers: Structural Design Group.
Client: TV Asahi. **Gross floor area:** 73,700 m². **Materials:** steel Vierendeel truss system, aluminum curtain wall, steel louvers, reinforced concrete.

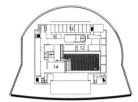

Glazing coat
ARCHITECTS: Maki and Associates

The glass-walled atrium of the new headquarters of TV Asahi, the icon of the project, acts as an interface between the public and private domains. The 30-meter high, 120-meter long Vierendeel frames form a gentle curve that follows the path of adjacent streets. The ladder-like steel units are factory welded and joined together on site using custom mechanical joints, comprised of vertical and horizontal pins, eccentric rings and Spiro locks. The transparent atrium becomes an active urban space, together with the front garden and adjacent squares animated with art pieces by Martin Puryear and Tatsuo Miyajima. The west and east façades are veiled with louvered screens that filter direct sunlight while creating an ephemeral silhouette resembling a large Japanese lantern in the evening.

01 Plans and section **02** View of atrium from the second floor **03** Aerial night view

Trade Fair Center Basel, Hall 1, 1999
Address: Messeplatz, Basel, Switzerland. **General contractor:** ARGE Preiswerk / Steiner. **Client:** MCH Messe Schweiz AG, Basel. **Gross floor area:** 62,500 m². **Materials:** concrete, glass, steel.

Inside – outside

ARCHITECTS: Theo Hotz Architekten + Planer

The new exhibition hall 1 consists of two superimposed halls, each measuring 18,000 square meters. The hall is located across the street from smaller residential units, which are reflected in the 20-meter high hall façade. The building's specific character lies in its double façade. The inner and outer longitudinal façades are six meters apart, creating a spatial and thermal buffer. The concentration of all service functions like service elevator, the air conditioning plant, switch rooms, emergency stairs, bathrooms, etc. in this buffer zone frees the interior hall of all obstacles. The building's transparent envelope creates an exciting contrast of design next to the simple frame, and the façade's transparency enables the visitor to gain a visual reference to the external world, and vice versa. The building was erected in only seven months between the annual watch and jewelry fair.

07

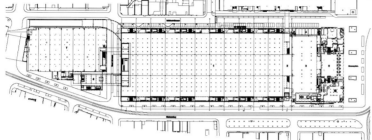

08

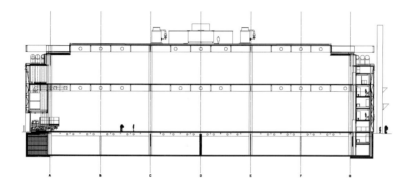

09

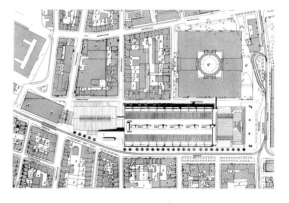

Wellness center "Tschuggen Berg Oase", 2006
Address: Tschuggen Grand Hotel, Arosa, Switzerland.
Civil engineers: Fanzun AG. **Light planning:** Büro für innovative Lichtplanung, Jürgen Häcker. **Client:** Tschuggen Grand Hotel, AG Grandhotel Tschuggen.
Gross floor area: 5,300 m². **Materials:** glass, Duke white granite, Canadian maple wood, titan zinc.

Lancet tree

ARCHITECTS: Mario Botta

Arosa offers an extraordinary geographic configuration of a natural water basin surrounded by mountains. The spa is next to the Tschuggen Grand Hotel, which is linked to it by a three-layered glass bridge. The aim was to 'build without building', to assert the presence of the new through the emergent parts of the skylights (so-called "trees of light") and to leave the great volume with the functional program intact. The inner space, distributed on four levels, appears as a terraced continuum with the slope. The different areas of the Berg Oase are characterized by their interrelation and privileged relationship with the environment. The outdoor spaces (sauna, solarium, swimming pool) are reachable directly from the pool and are set on a terracing jutting into the surrounding nature.

02

04

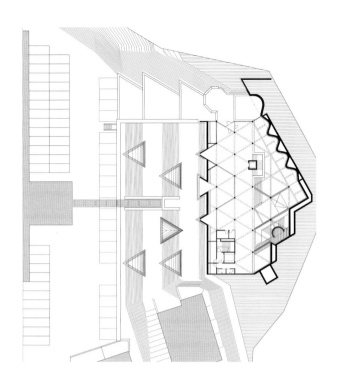

05

06

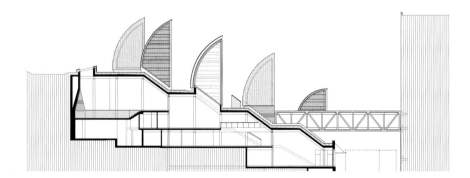

Library Technical University Delft, 1998
Address: Library Technical University Delft, Pro-
metheusplein 1, Delft, The Netherlands. **Client:** ING
Real Estate, Den Haag; Technische Universiteit
Delft. **Gross floor area:** 15,000 m². **Materials:** glass,
grass, concrete, metal, wood.

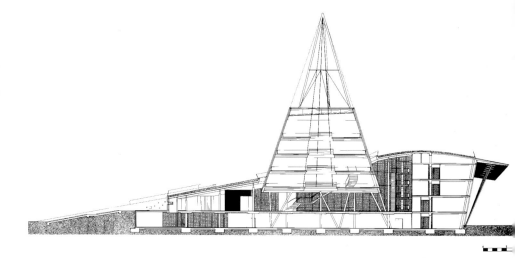

Building as landscape
ARCHITECTS: Mecanoo architecten

The library is a building which wants to be a landscape.
The lawn is lifted on one of its sides like a sheet of pa-
per, and columns are placed beneath, with glass walls
between them: this is a building of grass and glass. It
is a landscape of gently curving shapes, whose edges
are the only sharp elements. One can literally walk over
the library, and a large volume was needed to stand in
contrast to the landscape: a cone, which gives shape
to the round, introverted reading rooms was placed on
top of the building. The rooms are suspended from the
apex of the cone, giving the hall a large support-free
space. The cone is a symbol of technology, but it also
stands for calm and contemplation. Like a drawing pin,
it holds down the landscape's endless form.

01 Section **02** Library entrance **03** East wing with offices

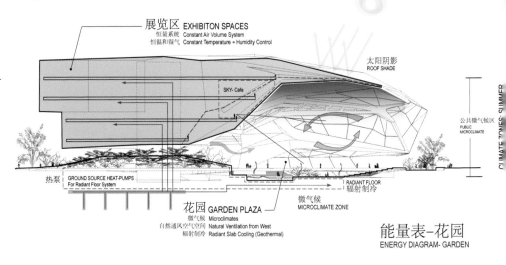

展览区 EXHIBITON SPACES
恒量系统 Constant Air Volume System
恒温和湿气 Constant Temperature + Humidity Control

太阳阴影
ROOF SHADE

SKY- Cafe

公共微气候区
PUBLIC
MICROCLIMATE

热泵 GROUND SOURCE HEAT-PUMPS
For Radiant Floor System

RADIANT FLOOR
辐射制冷

CLIMATE ZONES- SUMMER

花园 GARDEN PLAZA
微气候 Microclimates
自然通风空气空间 Natural Ventilation from West
辐射制冷 Radiant Slab Cooling (Geothermal)

微气候
MICROCLIMATE ZONE

能量表-花园
ENERGY DIAGRAM- GARDEN

Shenzhen Museum of Contemporary Art, 2007
Address: Shenzen, China. **Client:** Shenzhen munici-pal government. **Gross floor area:** 28,000 m². **Materials:** glass.

Lily pad plaza

ARCHITECTS: Emergent

In order to delimit and intensify the site conditions, the building massing is designed as a mirror reflection of the L-shaped YAH building to the north. A garden plaza is located in the void created by the L-shape, which serves as a meeting point and gateway to the cultural delights offered inside the new building. The plaza roof offers shade, while plant life and water features cool the air below based on principles of natural convection and evaporative cooling, creating a thermally regulated environment. The building structure spreads over architectural surfaces according to load paths, driven by a rule-based system of branching and computational subdivision like the veins of a lily pad forming a semi-monocoque.

01 Energy diagram **02** Lobby interior **03** General view

Residential house S108, 2006
Address: Germany. **Client:** private. **Gross floor area:** 310 m². **Materials:** ferroconcrete, stonework, aluminum and glass façade, sunscreen between glass panes.

Osmotic living

ARCHITECTS: steimle architekten

The compact house, whose exterior is completely glazed on three sides, emerges intentionally as an independent volume within its surroundings thanks to its volume and exact, clear outlines. The glass façade is merely a necessary thermal membrane separating the exterior and the interior, cold and warmth. The special features of the location enable views of surrounding nature in a widescreen format. Using full-height glass sliding doors, open spaces like terraces and gardens at varying heights are brought directly into the living space. On the southern side, the glass façade enables passive absorption of solar energy during the cold season. Projecting balconies, a wide roof overhang and sun protection systems located in the panels' inner spaces prevent overheating in the summer.

04

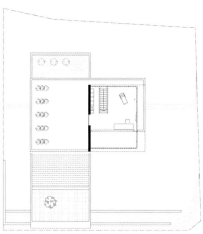

05

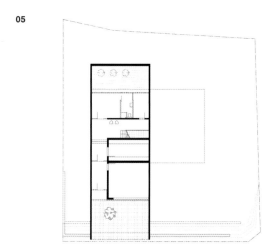

06

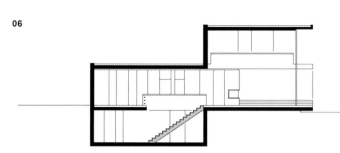

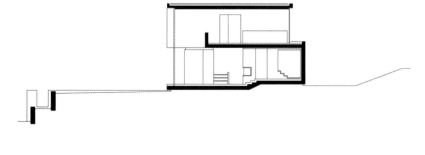

07

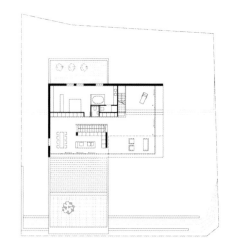

08

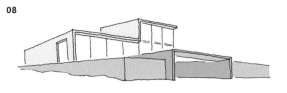

9

Holmes Place, Shellmex house, 2001
Address: Shellmex house, The Strand, London, WC1,
UK. **Client:** Holmes Place. **Gross floor area:** 3,200 m².
Materials: glass, stainless steel, slate stone, corian,
timber, plaster.

Light-therapy

ARCHITECTS: ORMS Architecture and Design

Located in a listed building from the early 20th century,
the club fully utilizes existing space and form to create a social hub in the heart of London's busy West
End. The club occupies three floors, starting from the
Strand entrance level and continuing down. The swimming pool is in a double-height space viewable from
the clubroom, acting as the club's focal point from the
mezzanine level. Reception is located on the restruc-
tured mezzanine and viewed from the entrance lobby
at the Strand level. A series of treatment rooms is also
located at this level. The design takes visitors down
into the heart of the building and offers views and
glimpses that link the internal spaces, bringing together the club's elements. Glass is used extensively to
create views and to ensure visual connection throughout. Colored glass and screening applied to it create
a sense of energy while providing privacy to spaces
when needed.

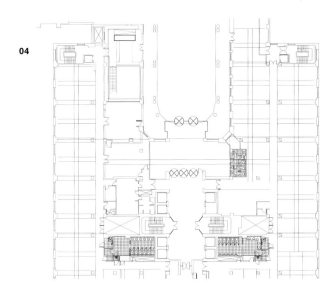

04

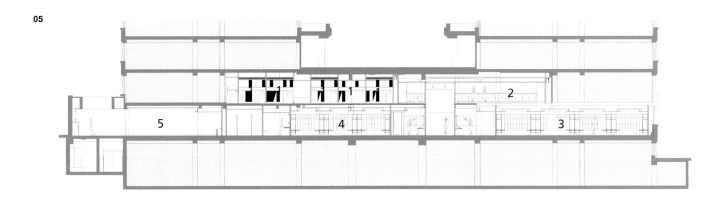

05

06

01

Roman Museum in the Xanten archeological park, 2008
Address: Archäologischer Park Xanten, Siegfried-straße 39, Xanten, Germany. **Artist:** Thomas Weil. **Client:** Landschaftsverband Rheinland. **Gross floor area:** 4,873 m². **Materials:** steel, glass, aluminum.

On historic grounds
ARCHITECTS: GATERMANN + SCHOSSIG

The museum building is built on the foundations of the former thermal hall. The spatial concept recreates the historical proportions – the main structure standing on the historical walls consists of box-shaped, meter-deep steel frames. Due to the perspective compaction of the frames, the view upon entering the museum recreates the original massive space. Vertically ordered panels with integrated glazing create the outer envelope of the museum. The exhibition level, a filigree steel construction suspended from the framework, is designed as a surface continuum developed in space. The layer development in the vertical dimension is experienced as a walkable "time strip", presenting the exhibition as a historical journey through the Roman period.

02

03

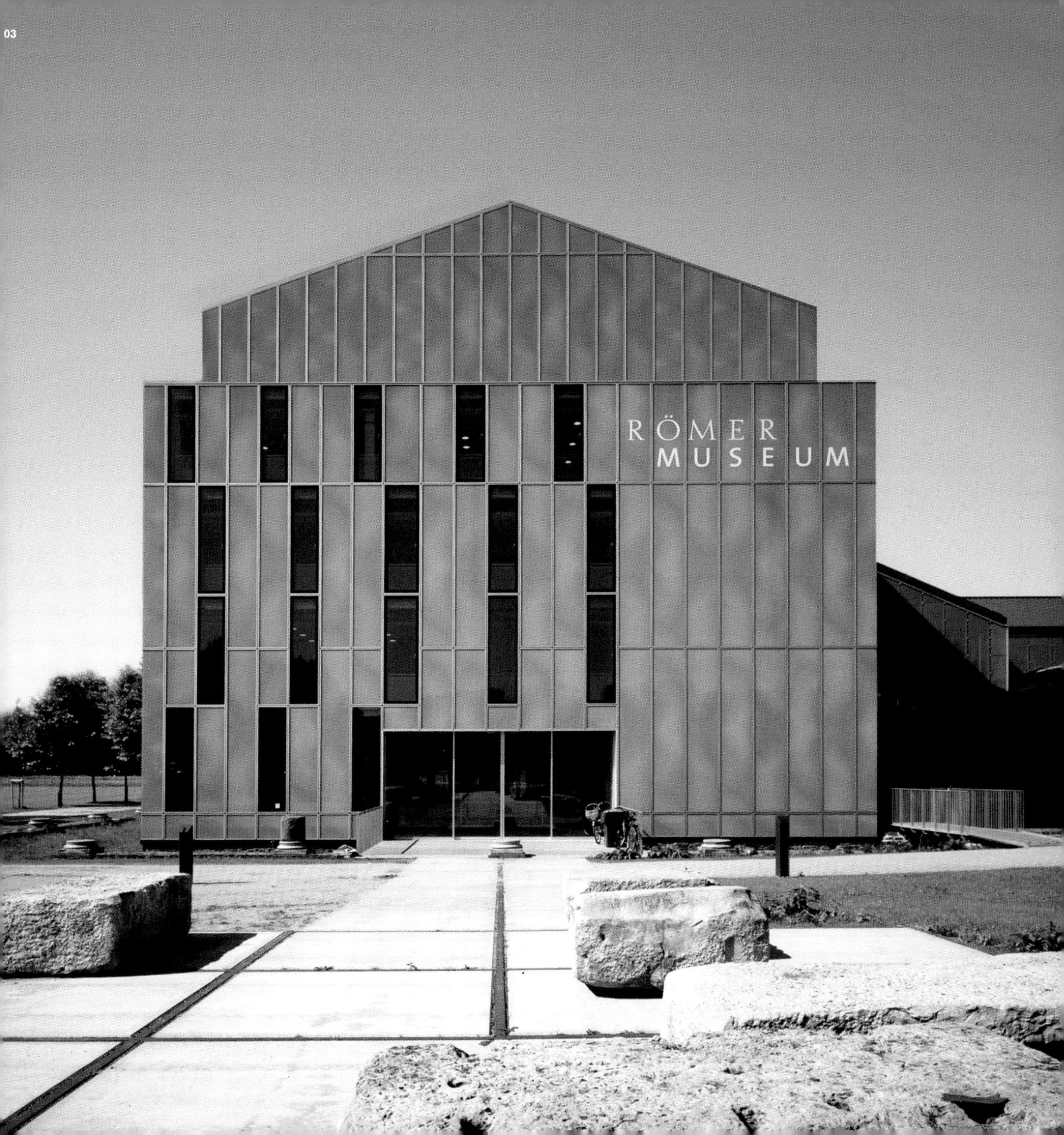

04

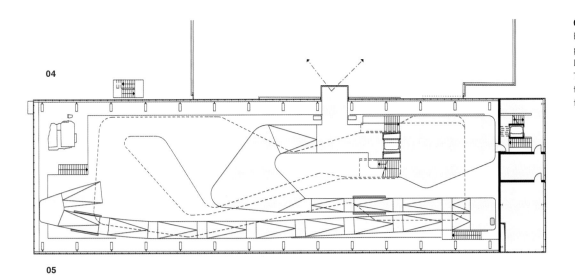

05

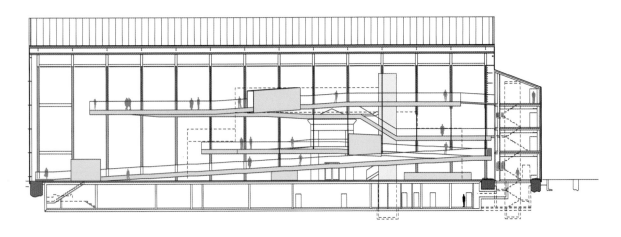

06

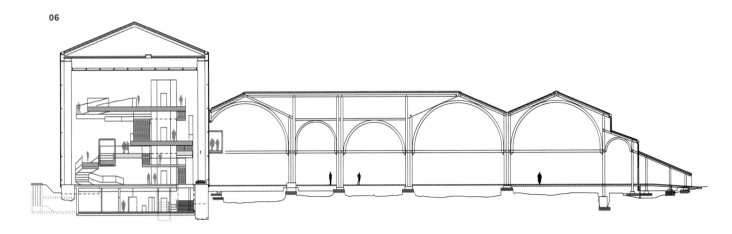

01

Alpbach Congress Center, 1999
Address: Alpbach, Tirol, Austria. **Client:** Alpbach Tourismus GmbH. **Gross floor area:** 2,200 m². **Materials:** glass, loam, concrete, steel, wood, sandstone.

Glassed cave

ARCHITECTS: conrad messner - markus prackwieser - othmar zobl / Architekturwerkstatt din a4

The building is gently fit into its geographical and natural surroundings and offers a view of the town and countryside, featuring farms and mountains. Clear structures are used to define space. Conference rooms, directly developed from the street, are laid out on two levels and are connected by a central lobby. The glass spiral forms the center of the building's first level and represents the main characteristic feature of the façade on the edge of the second level. It symbolizes an acoustic perception of the legendary Ear of Dionysius' cave and a mouthpiece of intellectual ideas. The clay wall, a natural regulator for climate and living conditions, describes a symbiosis between the building and its environment.

02

03

04

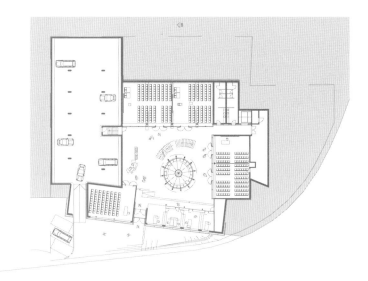

05

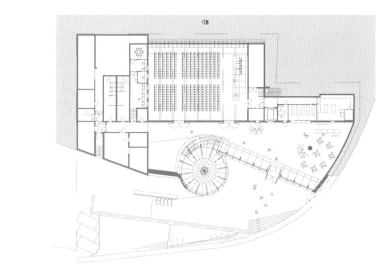

06

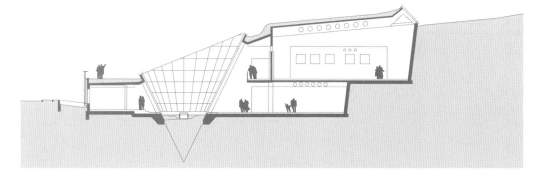

Norddeutsche Landesbank, 2002
Address: Am Friedrichswall 10, Hanover, Germany.
Structural engineers: Wetzel & v. Seht with Pfef-
ferkorn & Partner. **Landscape architects:** Nagel &
Schonhoff. **Energy concept:** Transsolar. **Client:**
Norddeutsche Landesbank Hanover. **Gross floor area:**
75,000 m². **Materials:** reinforced concrete, glass, wood,
carpet.

Detached from the block
ARCHITECTS: Behnisch Architekten

The new building of the Norddeutsche Landesbank
(North German Federal Bank) can be found at the intersection of a Hanover commercial center and the
residential areas in the southern section of the city.
The street spaces are stabilized using a perimeter
development, typical for the city, which reacts to the
surroundings with its height. The desired mixture of
residential and commercial space is achieved on the
ground level, where a readily accessible, public area
with restaurants, cafes and stores was created. The
80-meter high house projects out of the perimeter
development. It continues freely according to its own
measures of scale and takes a superordinate relation
to the neighborhood. Due to its generous glazed sections, the building appears light in spite of its size.

02

3

04

05

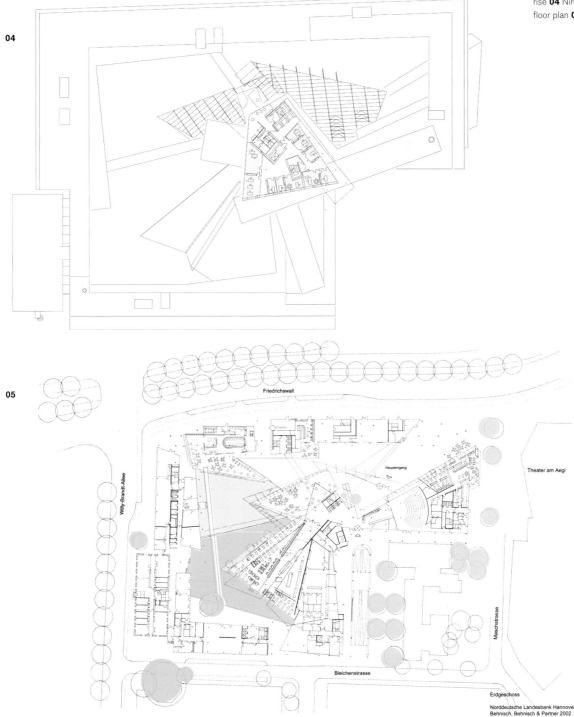

Friedrichswall

Willy-Brandt-Allee

Haupteingang

Theater am Aegi

Maschstrasse

Bleichenstrasse

Erdgeschoss

Norddeutsche Landesbank Hannover
Behnisch, Behnisch & Partner 2002

Nokia Research Center, 1999
Address: Itämerenkatu 11–13, Helsinki, Finland.
Client: Nokia Company. **Gross floor area:** 35,650 m².
Materials: glass, metal, steel-coated mineral wood elements.

Glass at its nimblest

ARCHITECTS: Tuomo Siitonen and
Esko Valkama / Helin & Siitonen Architects

The Nokia Research Center is a flexible office building which also contains subdivided rooms. The building accommodates various ever-changing functions of a research center ranging from office work to electronics laboratories, but eliminates the need to physically alter the building. At the center of the building is a tall atrium surrounded by glass-walled offices looking inside. The main external cladding material is glass, and the metal parts of the building's "rain coat" are minimized. The top of the intermediate space in the double façade is provided with an adjustable louver, while the bottom is left open. The actual heat-insulating envelope is built of light steel-coated mineral wood elements and fixed wood framed windows. The bolted façade sections can be detached and recycled.

04

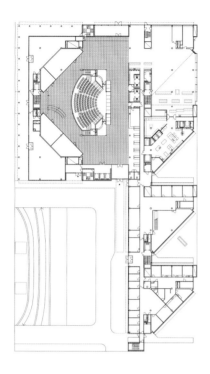

06

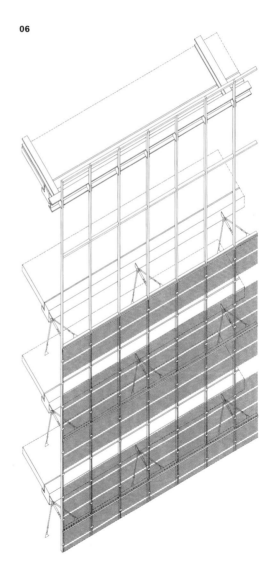

05

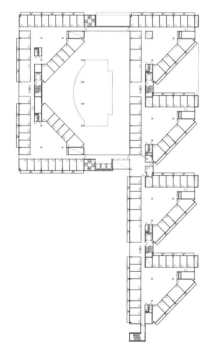

7

London City Hall, 2002
Address: Greater London Authority City Hall, The Queen's Walk, London, United Kingdom. **Structural engineers:** Arup, Davis Langdon & Everest. **Lanscape architects:** Arup Townshend Landscape Architects, The Fountain Workshop Ltd. **Light planning:** Claude Engle Lighting, Equation Lighting Design Ltd. **Client:** More London Development Ltd. **Materials:** glass, steel, concrete.

Demoglassy

ARCHITECTS: Foster + Partners

City Hall houses the assembly chamber for the members of the London Assembly and the offices of the mayor and staff of the Greater London Authority. The City Hall expresses the transparency and accessibility of the democratic process and demonstrates the potential for a sustainable, virtually non-polluting public building. The shape achieves optimum energy performance by minimizing the surface area exposed to direct sunlight. A range of active and passive shading devices is also employed: to the south the building leans back so that its floor-plates step inwards to provide shading for the naturally ventilated offices. The chamber faces north across the river to the Tower of London, its glass enclosure allowing Londoners to see the Assembly at work. At its base, opening on to a piazza is a cafe overlooking the river; and from the entrance foyer, gentle ramps allow visitors to move up through the building.

01 Spiral **02** General view, Thamse
on the left side **03** Sketch **04** Cross
section **05** Conference room

03

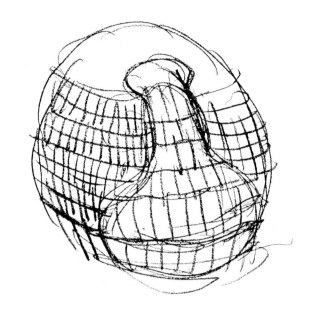

04

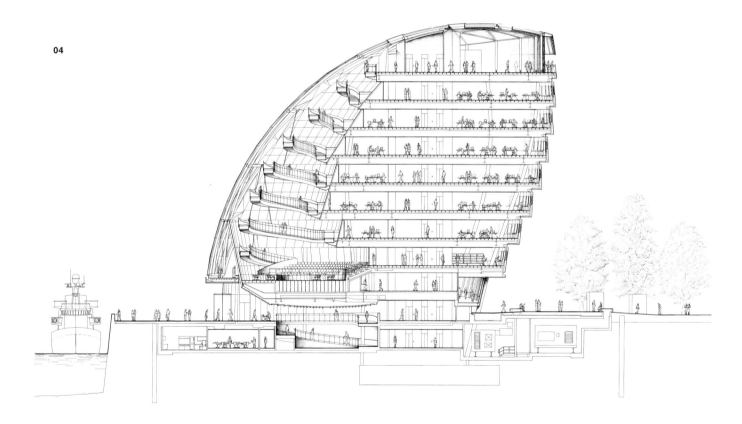

05

**Administrative and educational center
Weishaupt AG, 1999**
Address: Chrummacherstrasse 8, Geroldswil, Switzer-
land. **Project management:** Perolini Baumanagement AG.
Client: Weishaupt Max GmbH, Schwendi, Germany.
Gross floor area: 4,075 m². **Materials:** concrete, steel,
glass, natural stone.

Crystal noise

ARCHITECTS: Theo Hotz Architekten + Planer

A 45-meter long and 13-meter high glazed noise and sun
protection shield erected along the highway boundary
acts as a conceptual, design and functional backbone
of the building's external shell. Born of the idea for an
oversized "crystalline" screen, the shield unifies the
various parts of the building into a meaningful whole,
simultaneously playing with the different façade layers
that come in contact with the shield. The high proportion
of glass found in the building reflects the wish for the
highest level of outer and inner transparency. Even at
night, through artificial illumination, the building retains
its attractive appearance. As a prominent element to
the complex hangs on the shield the name "Weishaupt"
successfully advertising the firm and its products on
one of the busiest highways in Switzerland.

03

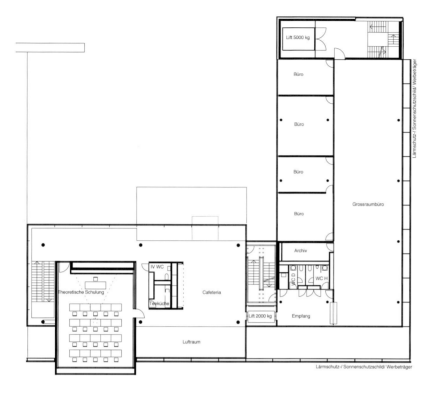

01 Interior view **02** Front view **03** First floor plan **04** Cross section **05** South-east view **06** East view, offices

04

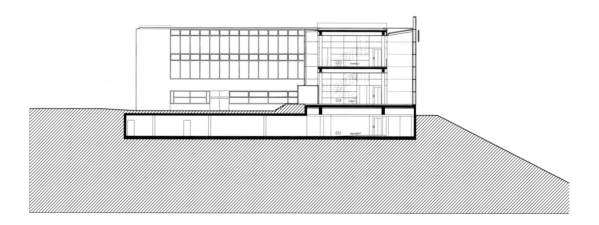

Dutch pavilion World Expo 1998
Address: Lisbon, Portugal. **Graphics:** Total Design.
Constructor: ABT. **Client:** Foundation Netherland
World Fairs. **Gross floor area:** 1,475 m². **Materials:**
steel and multi-layered harded and colored glass with
texture.

Breaking waves

ARCHITECTS: Paul Wintermans /
Quist Wintermans Architekten

The Dutch pavilion of the Lisbon Expo views the
oceans as our heritage for the future. The exhibition
hall was spatially divided by means of a centrally located element in the form of a dike, partially covered
with a glass wave. Visitors enter below the glass wave,
move through a transparent hall and continue on their
way up an asphalt slope to the top of the dike. Once
there, an overview of the whole exhibition opens to
their eyes. Above the wave is an enormous projection
screen, consisting of nine square elements placed
next to one another, on which changing pictures are
projected. The exhibition deals with a large number of
subjects relating to the Netherlands' location on the
North Sea.

01 On the dike, looking at the wave **02** Under the glass wave **03** Right side wave **04** Drawing, cross section pavilion **05** Drawing, plan pavilion black and white **06** Left of the wave

04

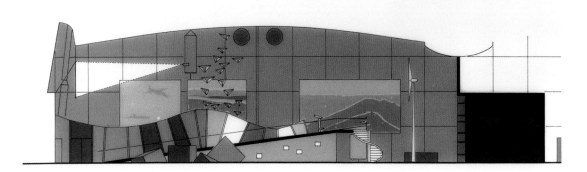

05

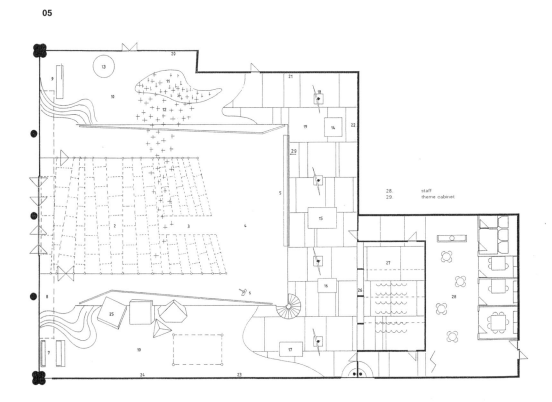

28. staff
29. theme cabinet

06

Uma Ilha Holandesa do mar de Wadden

A Dutch Wadden Sea Island

del mar de les Wadden

Polders construídos num delta fluvial

Polders in a river delta

Polders em um delta del río

Sony Center, 2000
Address: Potsdamer Straße, Berlin, Germany. **Structural engineers:** Ove Arup New York, BGS Ingenieursozietät. **Special structures:** Werner Sobek Ingenieure. **Light-art:** AIK / Yann Kersale (Forum & Gates), Vincennes. **Client:** Sony, TishmanSpeyer Properties, Kajima. **Gross floor area:** 132,500 m². **Materials:** glass, steel.

Scheerbarts glass and Tauts crown

ARCHITECTS: Murphy / Jahn

The exterior of the multifunctional center is a part of the reconstructed Berlin, while its interior is a city in its own right. With its characteristics of transparency, permeability to light and reflection and refraction, there is a constant change of imagery and effects during both day and night. The main office buildings are located at each corner of the site. Their surfaces employ sophisticated glass and lightweight steel technologies. The façades of the corner office buildings are constructed with load-bearing glass mullions. The Esplanade Residence incorporates historic and salvageable parts of the landmark Esplanade Hotel that are displayed behind a large cable-supported glass screen, as if inside a large shop case.

01 Façade with balconies **02** The "Esplanade Residence" **03** View inside **04** Cross section **05** Façade system **06** Roof **07** Corridor **08** Façade outside

04

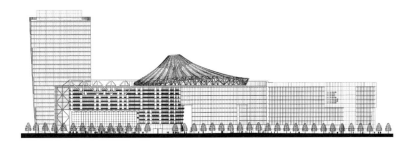

05

06

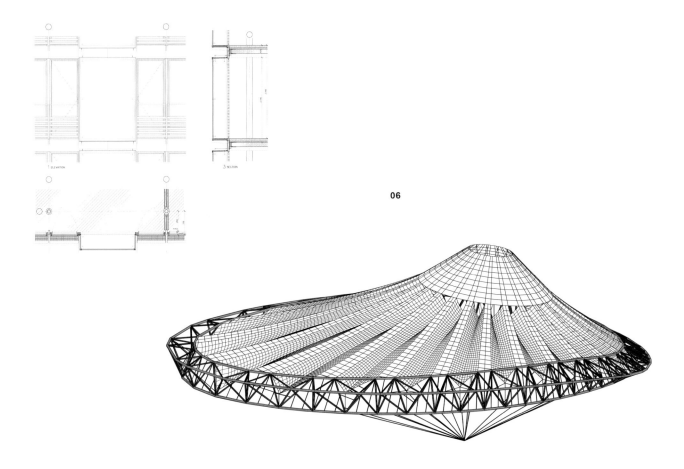

MANIFEST

R3 ukishima/aicafe 54, 2007
Address: 2-1-13 Matsuo, Naha-shi, Okinawa, Japan.
Client: Risa Partners Inc. **Gross floor area:** 492 m².
Materials: glass, steel, perforated concrete block screen.

Small flowers crack concrete

ARCHITECTS: Klein Dytham architecture

The four-unit commercial building is located just off Kokusai Dori, the location of many trendy boutiques and galleries, where Okinawa's tradition and young culture meet. The site had a long street frontage facing the side of a bland convenience store. All four retail units, including the café, would have had this as their view. A 25-meter long, five-meter high perforated concrete block screen, ubiquitous to Okinawa, was erected, enclosing a balcony access to the second floor while screening off the convenience store and electrical and telephone wires running along the street. The screen with its pixilated pink orchid pattern creates an encapsulated world for the café while letting air and light into the building.

03

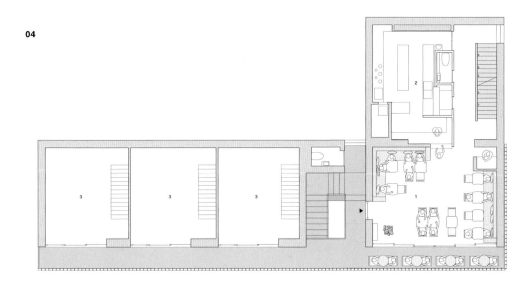

01 + 02 Night view **03** First floor plan **04** Second floor plan **05** Corridor **06** Interior

04

GO-House, 2006
Address: Thionville en Moselle, France. **Client:**
private. **Gross floor area:** 310 m². **Materials:** glass-
elements, metal, concrete (basement), zinc (roof).

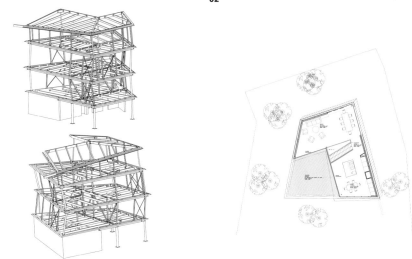

Glass bellows

ARCHITECTS: Periphériques (Marin-Trottin)

Organized in three levels over a below-ground parking garage, the building has outline glass "profilit" façades that offer thermal isolation as well as intimacy
protection. This translucent envelope is slanted and
the levels are shifted in relation to each other. The
windows in the walls behind the profilit panels often
do not follow their outline, being organized to best ac-
commodate the rooms and views from the house. A
zinc roof continues the glass wedge metaphor. The
house can be accessed from the street by a leaned
ramp; near the main door, a large stair leads to the
first floor, 4.5 meters above.

01 Construction **02** First floor plan **03** Bathroom **04** View from
the street

Offices Daimler Chrysler Financial Services, 2005
Address: Deventerlaan 101–121, Utrecht, The Netherlands. **Client:** IPMMC real estate development. **Gross
floor area:** 24,000 m². **Materials:** concrete, steel,
glass covered façades.

Hand in hand

ARCHITECTS: Meyer en Van Schooten

The urban plan and landscape design of the business
park where the new Daimler Chrysler buildings are
located incorporates a high density urban core with
offices and accommodations in a green setting. The
Daimler Chrysler buildings include offices, restaurant
and business accommodation. The two towers are the
highest buildings in the park. The transparent main
entrance is situated between the two towers and
gives access to both buildings and the underground
car parking. The overall layout is arranged in a clear
way to ensure floor plans which are highly functional
and flexible. The special glass façades give the buildings continuously changing layered effects of transparency and reflection of the surroundings.

01 View through the buildings
02 The two building volumes 03
South elevation section 04 West
elevation section 05 Interior view
of entrance hallway 06 Detail glass
façade

03

04

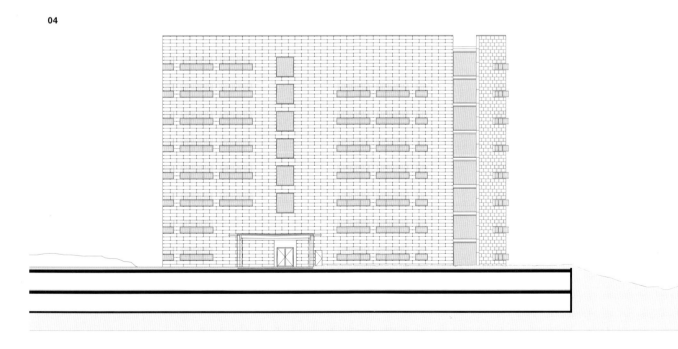

01

Residential house on Lake Zurich, 2000
Address: Seestrasse, Männedorf, Switzerland. **Client:** private. **Gross floor area:** 410 m². **Materials:** exposed concrete and frameless glazing in the stairway, glass, oiled Borneo teak, nero assoluto.

From black box to clear cube
ARCHITECTS: Bob Gysin + Partner BGP

The house is located on a plot between the highly-trafficked Seestrasse and Lake Zurich. The high quality of the lakeside views and optimal sun exposure have been used by creating a maximally transparent southern façade. On the north side, only one translucent glass cube breaks through the concrete envelope. At night, it appears as a lantern that marks the yard while illuminating it. The ground floor is designed as a large space, connected vertically to the work area on the top story via the gallery. The building is completely electronically connected – lighting, windows, sun protection and audio systems are automatically controlled. A ground probe warmth pump delivers heat energy and cools the structure in the summer.

02

04

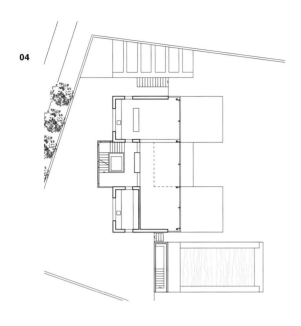

01 View from the lake **02** Stairway **03** Living room **04** Ground
floor plan **05** First floor plan **06**
Cross section **07** Attic floor plan
08 View from the street

05

06

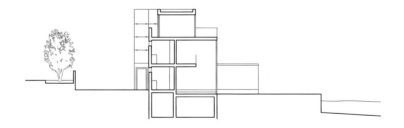

07

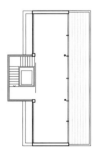

108

**Redesign House Building Society Wüstenrot AG –
headquarters, 2007**
Address: Alpenstraße 70, Salzburg, Austria. **Co-
Architects:** Dietmar Bach and Stephan Trauner.
Client: Bausparkasse Wüstenrot AG. **Gross floor
area:** 3,300 m². **Materials:** printed glass, different
dual-pane windows, flexible expanded metal façade.

Fine feathers make fine birds
ARCHITECTS: Strobl Architekten

This office building presents itself not only as an innovative prototype for ecological and energo-techni-
cal renovation, but is also a new attraction adorning
the entrance into the city together with a thought-
out greenery design. The suspended, stamped glass
façade creates an overall concept of the building's
"skin". The complex is clad in a transparent dress of
glimmering metal mesh lamellas, a modular system
of movable sun protection elements. The metal fabric
creates various light moods and presents the building
in a different optical view at different times of day –
from transparent to almost closed-off, from struc-
tured by deep folds to homogenously wrapped by
one surface.

04

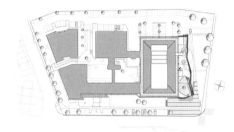

05

06

Factory TMS, 2007
Address: Carl-Zeiss-Straße 7–9, Saalfeld, Germany.
Team: Tobias Wenz (project architect), Philip Raum.
Contracting and property monitoring: Brückner
Ingenieure. **Structural engineers:** Hörnicke Hock
Thieroff. **Client:** TRUMPF Medizin Systeme GmbH.
Gross floor area: 2,500 m². **Materials:** aluminum,
glass, polycarbonate-elements.

Swinging with time
ARCHITECTS: Barkow Leibinger

The new building houses an installation/production
unit, offices, as well as new shower cabins and dressing rooms. A 6.5-meter high hall and a three-story
entrance hall containing offices and plumbing instal-
lations were added to existing building sections. Both
parts are encircled by an aluminum trapeze steel façade whose western side contains inserted floor-high
glass surfaces which provide impressive views of the
Saale River floodplain and Schlossberg. A polycarbon-
ate element band with a perforated trapeze steel sheet
acting as sun protection runs along the façade's lower
level. The roof structure consists of one spatial framework consisting of hollow profiles and diagonal round
beams which are integrated into the wide top illumination strip, filling the hall's 25-meter span.

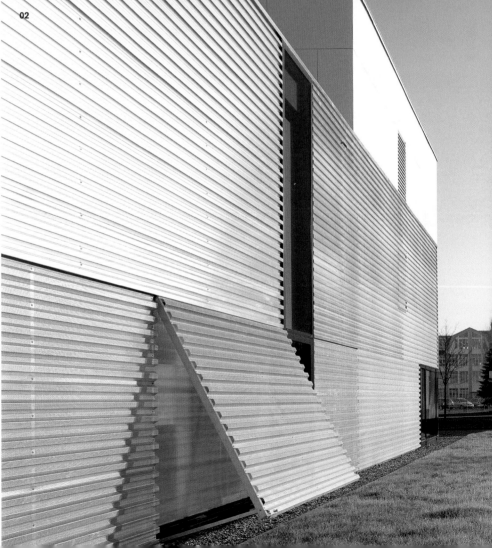

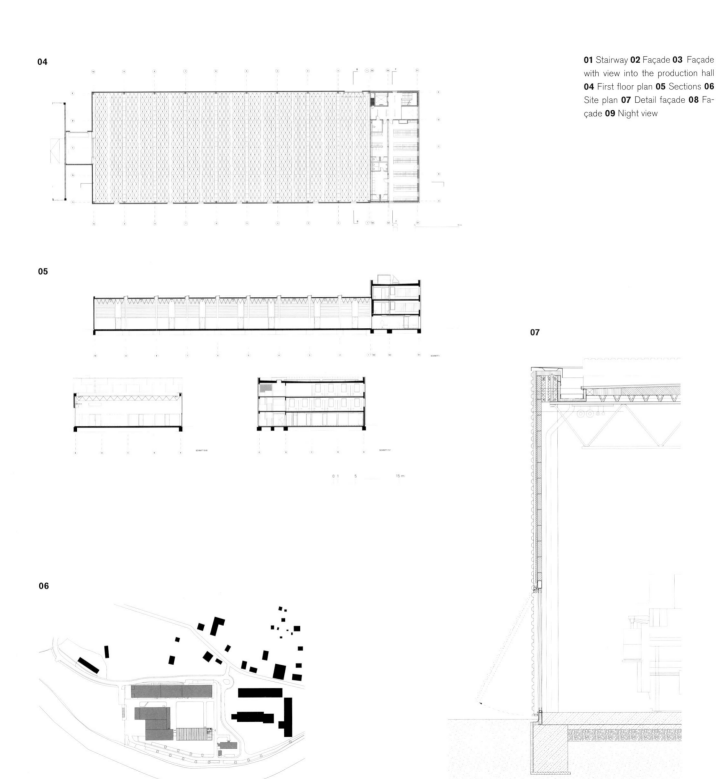

04

05

06

07

08

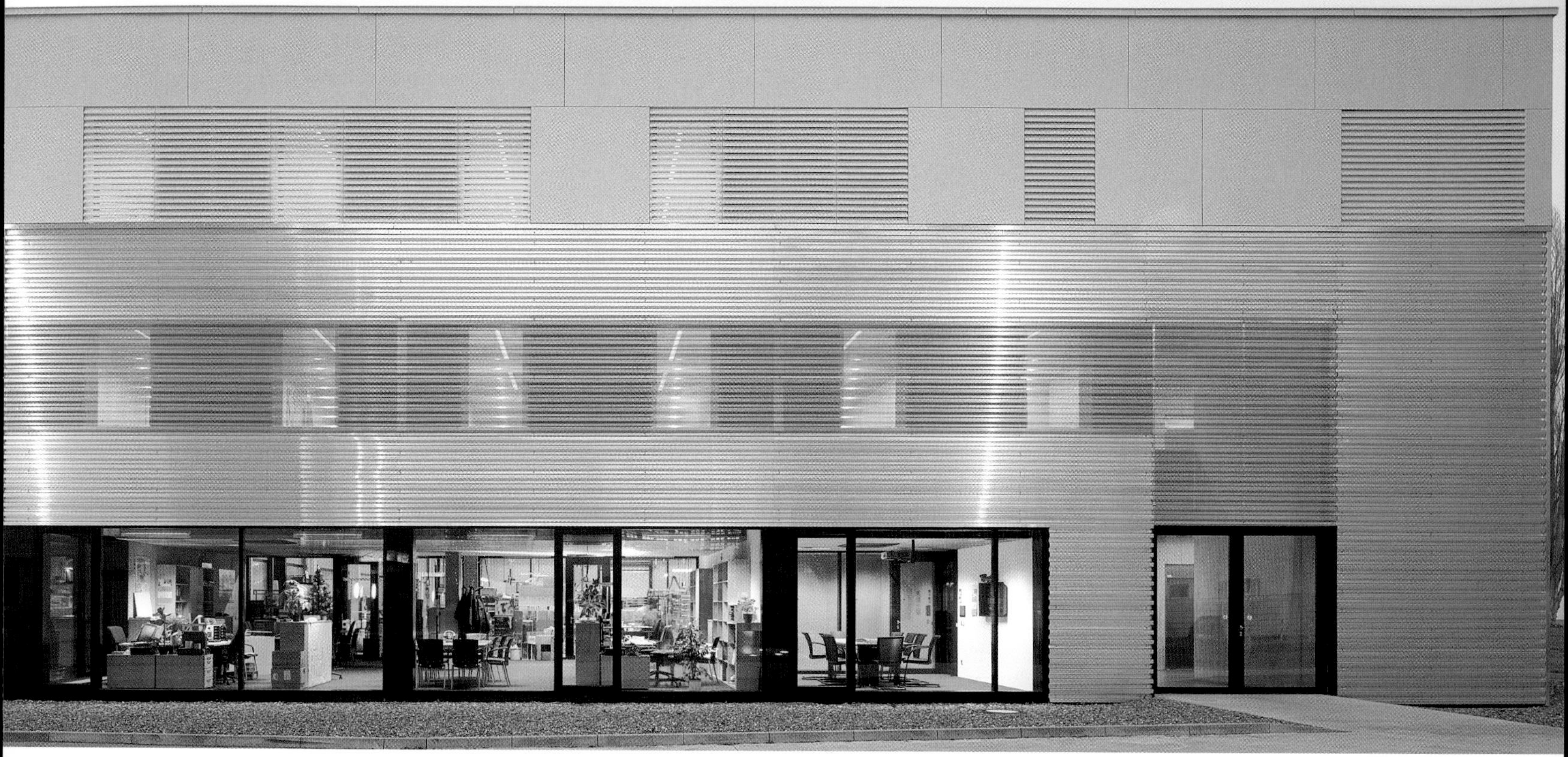

09

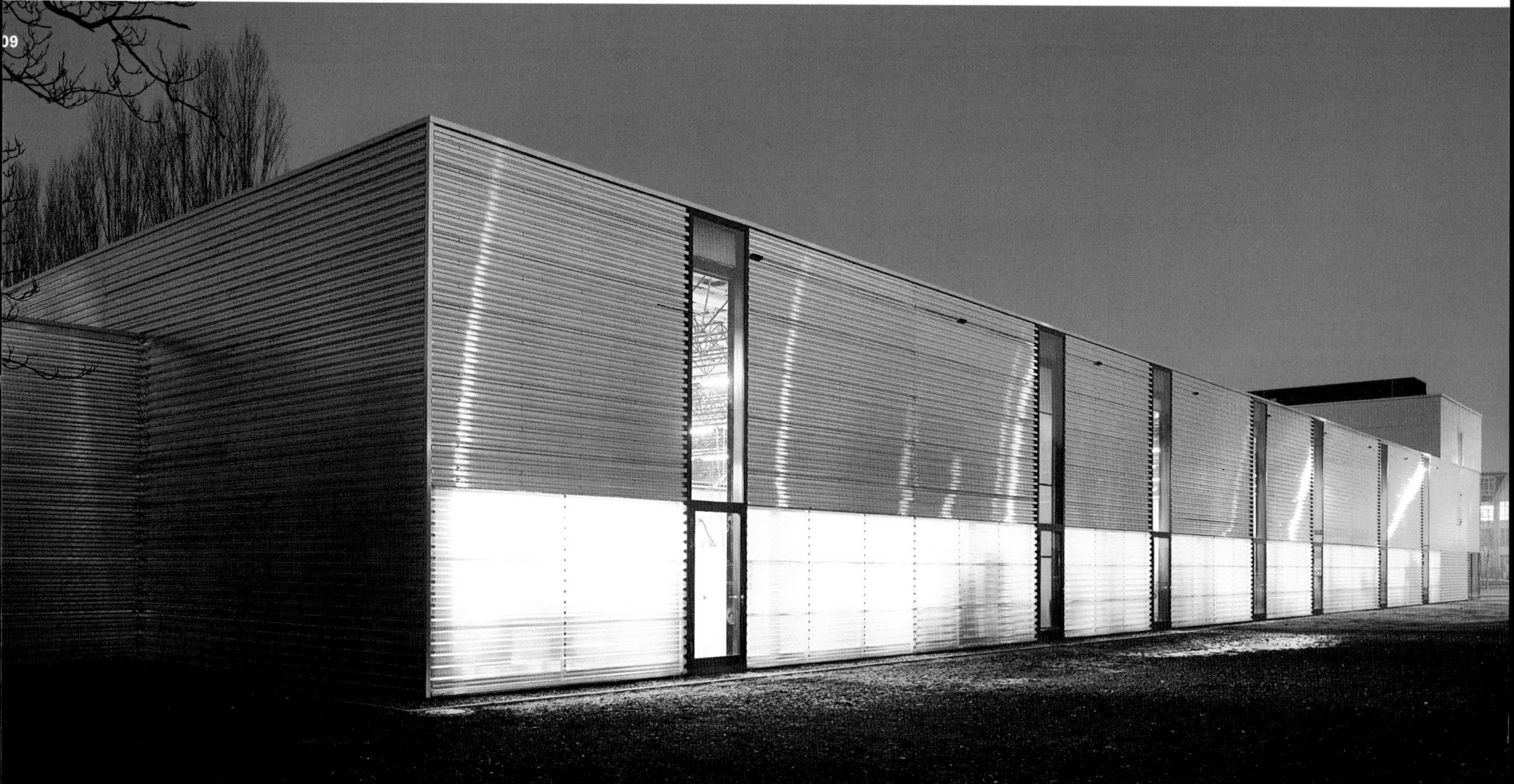

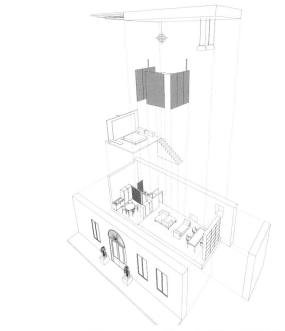

Trans-opaque loft, 2003
Address: Colonne Di San Lorenzo, Milan, Italy.
Client: Pier von Helfert. **Gross floor area:** 90 m².
Materials: glass, stone, wood.

Boundless living

ARCHITECTS: Pierfrancesco Cravel /
pfcarchitects

An empty long and narrow ground floor warehouse in
downtown Milan has been transformed into a home
with all necessary functions. Proceeding with a fun-
damental reconsideration of loft design, a white open
cube was created using white suspended ceilings and
vertical surfaces. To divide the space into three different areas, floating frosted glass panes were added. The
impression of the spacious room is retained thanks to
the translucent partitions. On the one hand, the divided
rooms flow seamlessly into one another, which is important for loft design; on the other, there is a physical
separation between the kitchen, bathroom and sleep-
ing area. To complete the loft character, the industrial
wooden floor was finished using a traditional smooth
white Beola stone in combination with resin.

01 Isometry **02** Kitchen **03** Bathroom **04** Living room

Commercial center, 2008
Address: Müllerstraße 36, Berlin, Germany. **Project leader:** Philipp Bauer. **Client:** Gutman Investment GmbH. **Gross floor area:** 4,331 m². **Materials:** metal, glass, plastering material.

Weddings' crystal heart

ARCHITECTS: Sergei Tchoban, nps tchoban voss GbR Architekten BDA
Alf M. Prasch Sergei Tchoban Ekkehard Voss

Observed from the street, the house appears crystal-like, as if growing out of the main thoroughfare and Wedding's central shopping street, its fully glazed façade contrasting against the stone-faced surroundings. Polygon-shaped folds acting as bays protrude up to 70 centimeters from the building's surface, alternating floor by floor. This prism-like surface produces variegated and unusual effects using reflections from the opposite side of the street, its passersby, the street surface and the sky. The interiors of the upper stories provide access to projecting façade sections located in the street's aerial space, offering views of the avenue continuing to the emblematic television tower on Alexanderplatz.

07

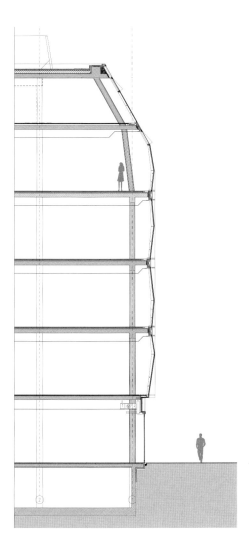

01 Detail façade **02** View from the side **03 + 04** Façade **05** Façade from the side **06** Night view **07** Section façade, street side **08** Street side view

08

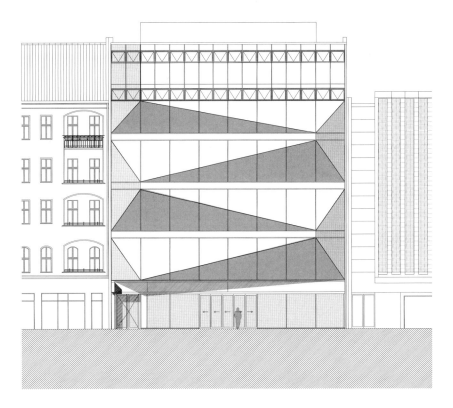

123

Twin Bricks house, 2008
Address: Saitama City, Japan. **Gross floor area:**
295 m². **Materials:** glass, glass bricks, steel, reinforced
concrete, autoclaced lightweight concrete-panels.

Phase-shifted

ARCHITECTS: Yasuhiro Yamashita,
Atelier Tekuto

Twin Bricks consists of two wings – five rental units
and the owner's two-family house. The owner's reinforced concrete wing stands closer to the road than
the rental wing with steel façades, ALC panels and
glass blocks. This building, based on the "Crystal
Brick" completed previously, enables these ALC panels to act as aseismatic elements in addition to the
glass blocks in order to improve cost effectiveness.
The physical similarity of glass blocks and ALC panels
was placed into focus, and this structure was realized
after a series of experiments. The contrast between
heavy and light versions of similar physicality and different material goes along with the spatial contrast,
making the space more exciting.

04

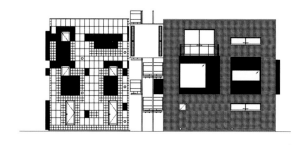

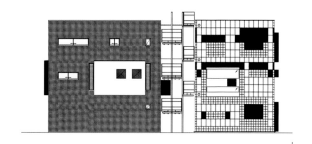

05

01

Pure glass tram stop on D-line, 2000
Address: Kattenbrookstrift 33, Hanover, Germany.
Glass engineers: Masche. **Art installation:** Despang
Architekten with Pit Schulz. **Structural engineers:**
ARUP Düsseldorf, Burmester und Sellmann Garbsen.
Dry construction system glass blocks: Steckfix. **Light
planning:** Fahlke & Dettmer Licht in der Architektur.
Client: Uestra Hanover / LBS. **Gross floor area:** 420 m²
platform. **Materials:** point-fixed safety glass as siding
around a steel construction.

Aire-opaque
ARCHITECTS: Despang Architekten

The waiting booths stand apart from their uniform
shape cannon chiefly through their choice of materials.
The two glass structures exemplify how their materiality interacts with the environment. The building em-
ploying glass stones alters its appearance depending
on the season and weather, transforming itself from
a cool monolith into a translucent, thin-skinned object,
revealing its inner structure due to its variable transparency. As the highlight of the structural progres-
sion, the counterpart consisting of plate glass demonstrates the series' tectonic inner life as a whole. This
elucidation, however, is continuously disguised by the
opaque randomly-generated fog. The small structures
custom-finished in a local Masche workshop vary in
their assembly and translucence.

Bischofshol /
Kinderkrankenhaus

04

07

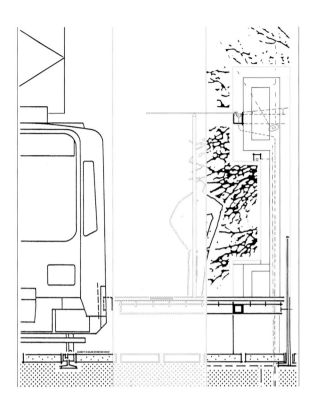

01 + 02 Night view from street side
03 Side view **04** Perspective **05 +**
06 Detail spot fixing **07** Section
08 Site plan **09** Arrangement of
the urban punctions

08

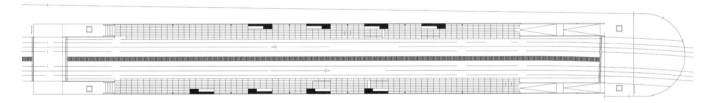

09

URBAN PUNCTIONS

White Ladybird house, 2008
Address: Shibuya Tokyo, Japan. **Gross floor area:**
172 m². **Materials:** glass, steel, reinforced, concrete.

Hip to be square

ARCHITECTS: Yasuhiro Yamashita,
Atelier Tekuto

The third creation from the Glass Block series employs steel-reinforced paneling. Everything was installed in the wall, which has a thickness of 95 millimeters. The 150 millimeters x 150 millimeters glass blocks and tiles appear seamlessly embedded in the wall during the daytime, and in the evening the light emanating from those points makes the whole space look like a glowing ladybird. The tiles used for the exterior walls were coated with "micro guard", a material developed in Japan with special techniques, preserving the beautiful condition of the walls for an extended time. The grid and texture of the walls become similar to that of the windows. The basement was designed to be easily expandable, allowing the owner to convert it into office or shop space.

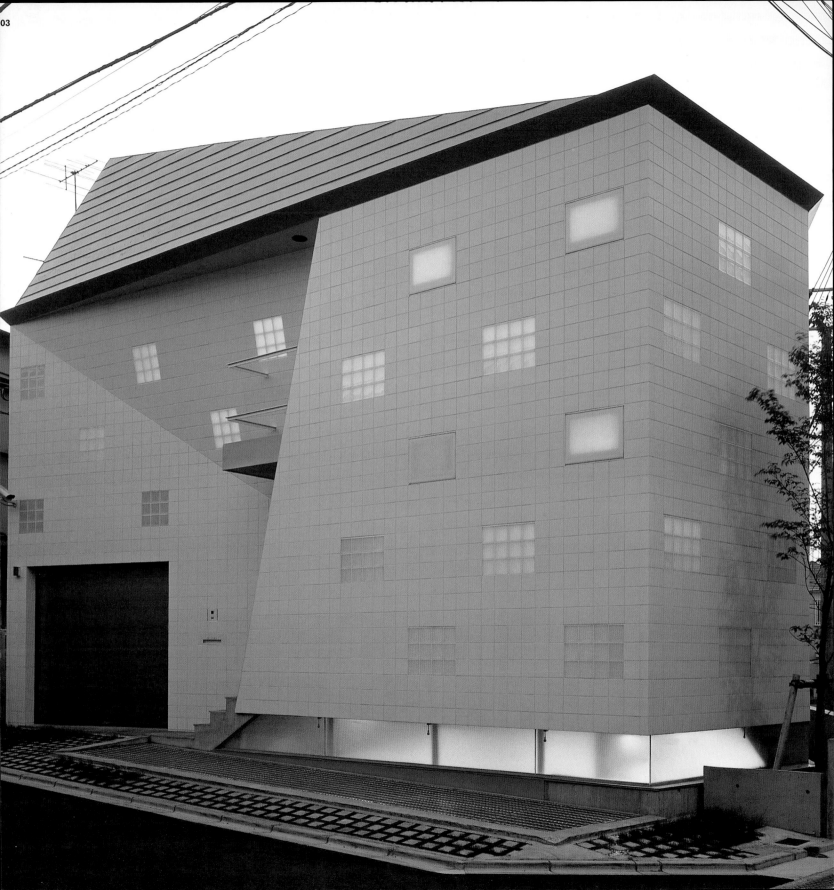

04

05

rooftop

Kitchen Dining Living 2,100

Parking space Private room Corridor 2,350 Stairs

Closet Basement 2,800 Closet

06

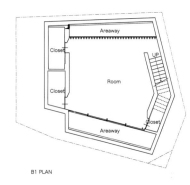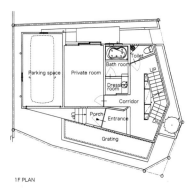

Areaway

Closet UP

Closet Room

Closet Areaway

B1 PLAN

Parking space Private room Bath room Toilet

Dressing room

UP

Corridor

Porch Entrance

Grating

1F PLAN

Terrace

Kitchen Dining Toilet

Living

Terrace DN

2F PLAN

134

Ponte de Lima municipal market, 2002
Address: Ponte de Lima, Portugal. **Structural engineers:** Proença e Neves. **Engineering:** Tomada Lda. **Main firm:** Teixeira Duarte, SA. **Client:** City Hall of Ponte de Lima. **Gross floor area:** 4,998 m². **Materials:** glass, wood, metal.

U-market

ARCHITECTS: José Guedes Cruz /
Guedes Cruz Arquitectos

The project to recover the market involved remodeling the existing buildings. With the replacement of two old wings by a new building, the market became U-shaped, opening the interior to the city and the river. The structure is punctuated by metallic frames, from which the wooden beams that uphold the glass roof covering the new square are suspended, providing the module with necessary rigidity. The structural materials mark the difference between what is permanent and what is transitory. The former, in traditional masonry, maintains its commitment to the site and guards against the violence of the river's floodwaters. The latter, made of wood and covered in copper and glass, breathes lightness and transparency, filling the square with light and shadow and bringing the traditional market to life.

04

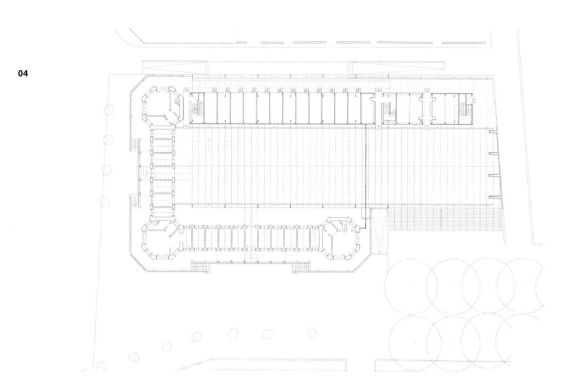

01 Exterior detail 02 Stairway 03 Exterior view 04 Ground floor plan 05 Longitudinal section 06 Cross section 07 Bird's eye view 08 Entrance detail

05

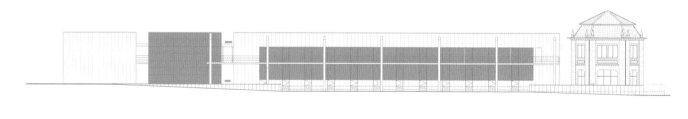

06

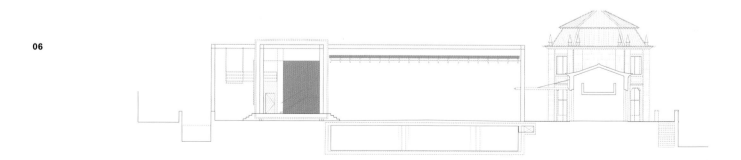

ARCA Regler GmbH – Innovation building, 2006
Address: Kempenerstraße 18, Tönisvorst, Germany.
Client: ARCA Regler GmbH. **Gross floor area:**
2,020 m². **Materials:** glass, steel, aluminum.

Skin on skin

ARCHITECTS: Anin · Jeromin · Fitilidis & Partner

Like a wide belt, the terrain winds its way along both side walls of the building toward the façade and intermingles with it. The front glass building houses the office premises, whereas the metallic building behind accommodates the development and production rooms. All supporting structures are made of visible steel beams, whose form describes the building's outline. Façade and interiors are made of individual elements so as to offer flexibility for modifications. Management area façade is made of two shells where the outside glass skin with an inclination of 55% is designed to keep out most of the solar radiation. Since the degree of incline varies and is lower at eye level, the office premises look extremely transparent and allow a good view outward.

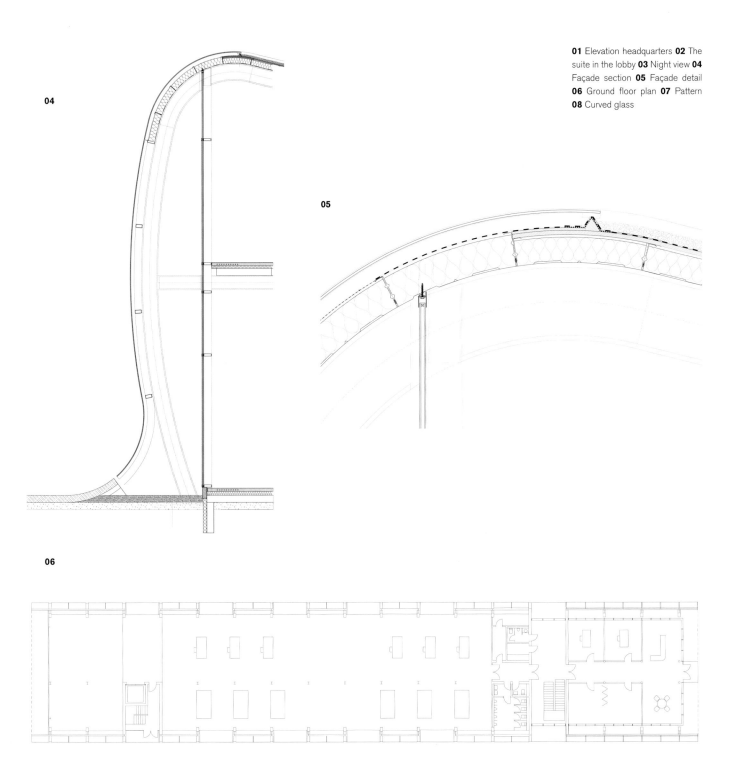

04

05

06

01

Kastrup switching station, 1999
Address: Kystvejen 3, Kastrup, Denmark. **Client:**
Københavns Energi. **Gross floor area:** 2,800 m².
Materials: in situ concrete, steel, aluminum, glass.

Put on the lights

ARCHITECTS: Gottlieb Paludan Architects

The context of the switching station has a significant influence on the design. Surrounded by traffic arteries near Copenhagen Airport, the switching station is seen from many angles and is in constant movement. Its circular shape reflects an attempt to release the structural geometry from the surroundings. The façade structure offers shifting images on different layers at different speeds. The outer layer consists of 2,496 panels – 1,345 x 586 x 12 millimeters clear, low-ferrous, tempered glass. Behind, two layers of expanded aluminum netting cover the entire façade, resulting in a distinctive moiré-effect. At night, the building appears to smolder. Each glass panel on the façade is fitted with fiber optic cables. From here, light travels through the glass to the frosted edge, where it is captured and diffused.

02

04

05

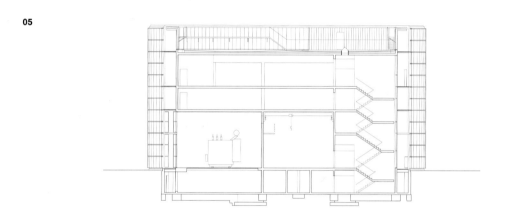

06

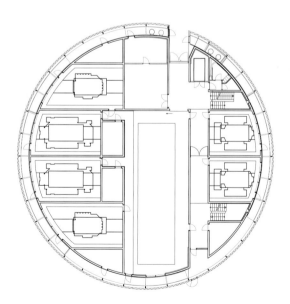

Chihuly bridge of glass, 2002
Address: Chihuly bridge of glass, 1801 Dock St, Tacoma, WA, USA. **Glass artist:** Chihuly Studio. **Project manager:** Adam Pyrek. **Client:** City of Tacoma - Tacoma, WA, USA. **Gross floor area:** 929,030 m². **Materials:** glacial blue polyvitro, concrete, balckened stainless steel, laminated glass panels.

Glass menagerie

ARCHITECTS: Andersson•Wise Architects

More than just a way to get from point A to point B, the bridge of glass is, in fact, an energized public experience. It was essential to allow visitors to pause, sit, look and be enveloped in Chihuly's art. Site-specific pavilions respond to the featured sculptures and objects, creating various worlds of Chihuly glass. The bridge provides a crucial pedestrian connection linking Tacoma's new Museum of Glass and the surrounding waterfront with the developing historic/cultural district. The bridge grows out of its material context of concrete and steel. Massive concrete supports and the painted steel superstructure have a powerful yet neutral presence that stands in contrast to Chihuly's artwork. The idea was not to compete for attention, but to create a prosaic counterpoint to the poetry of glass.

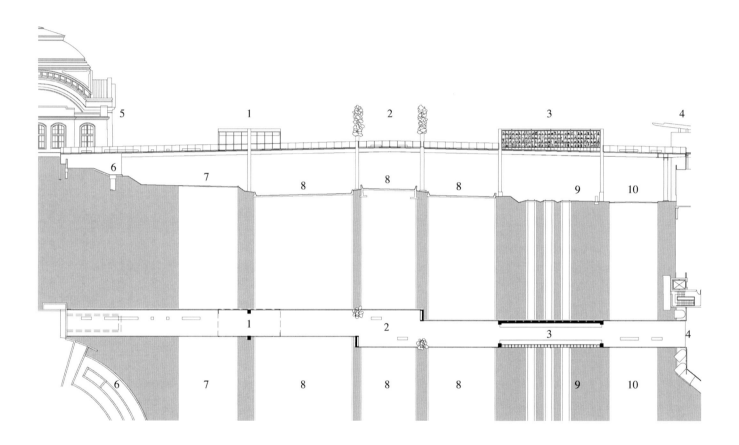

1. Seaform Pavilion
2. Crystal Gate
3. Venetian Wall
4. Museum of Glass by Others
5. Existing Union Station

6. Existing Washington State History Museum
7. Museum Parking
8. Interstate 705
9. Railroad Tracks
10. Dock Street

SECTION AND PLAN

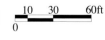

Lille Fine Arts Museum, 1997
Address: Place de la République, Lille, France.
Chandeliers: Gaëtano Pesce. **Atrium sculpture:**
Gulio Paolini. **Client:** City of Lille. **Gross floor area:**
28,000 m². **Materials:** toughened glass with a
printed mirror matrix on the inside, laminated clear
glass.

Flirting with the mirror image

ARCHITECTS: Jean Marc Ibos – Myrto Vitart
architects

The reflection realizes the interface between the old
and the new. In setting up infinities of depth, the mirror
articulates a continuum with the built environment. The
layered image of the palais and its monochromes, with
which the subject interacts as both voyeur and ac-
tor, symbolizes the museum within the city. The north
façade is composed of 416 panels. Each panel is a
double-glazed unit incorporating a printed matrix pattern. The supporting structure is composed of elliptical
polished stainless steel tubes. The courtyard side, the
"mirror wall", is cased with translucent glass to which
small mirror surfaces have been applied using screen
printing technique. Its intensive chrome character
generates a strong impressionist picture, making the
building appear nearly invisible.

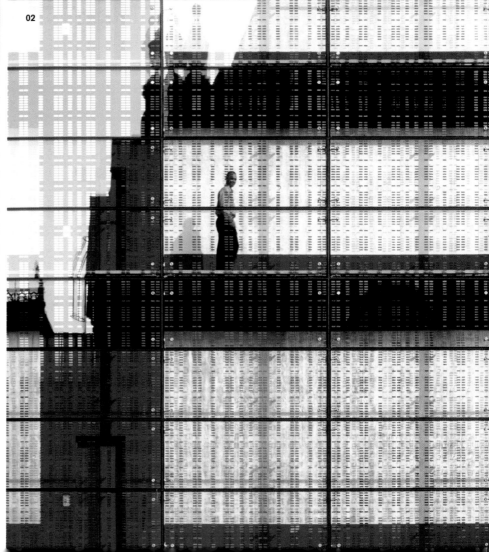

04

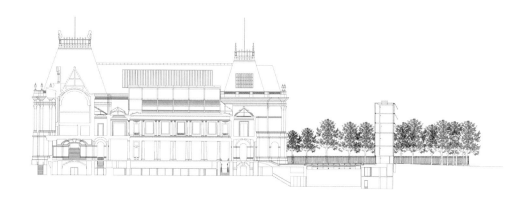

05

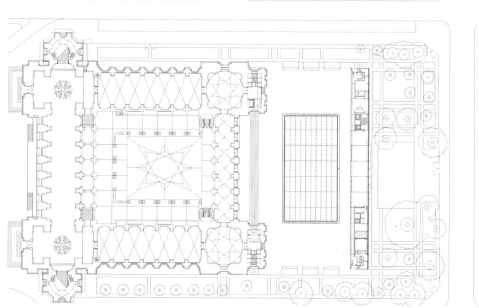

Administrative building "Korpus 25" renovation, 2008
Address: Swerdlowskaja-bank 44, Schukowa street. 1/2, Piskarewskij Prospect 4, Feodosijskaja street. 7, St. Petersburg, Russia. **Project leader:** Frederik S. Scholz. **Client:** Teorema. **Gross floor area:** 7,705 m². **Materials:** structural-glazing-façade with digital printed double glazing.

Ever-blooming façade

ARCHITECTS: Sergei Tchoban, nps tchoban voss GbR Architekten BDA
Alf M. Prasch Sergei Tchoban Ekkehard Voss

"Korpus 25" is located in a St. Petersburg park that formerly belonged to the tsars. Following the Russian revolution, this habitat was destroyed to a large extent by targeted relocation of industrial factories into the area. The building's frame remains a component of the post-revolutionary industrial architecture, with two additional stories stacked on top. The glass envelope is printed with summer leaves and flower motifs and presents itself as a reminiscence of the nature park that was once here. The building decorated along its almost complete surface offers inhabitants on the upper floors views through the openings in the floral design, while along the ground floor on the back façade, the building opens itself up through a fully glazed winter garden towards an old pond.

04

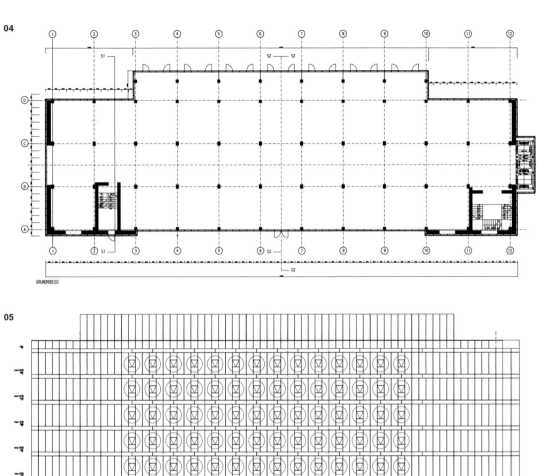

GRUNDRISS EG

01 View hatch **02** View fixed glazing **03** General view **04** Ground floor plan **05** Side elevation **06** Detailing façade **07** Flower curtain

05

06

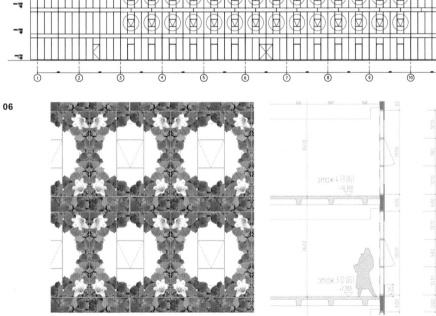

07

C42, Citroën flagship showroom, 2007
Address: 42, avenue des Champs-Élysées, Paris, France. **Project manager:** Anne Feldmann. **Structural engineers:** Khephren. **Fluid engineers:** Alto. **Multimedia engineers:** Labeyrie. **Client:** Automobiles Citroën. **Gross floor area:** 1,200 m². **Materials:** glass, steel, concrete.

Homage á Citroën

ARCHITECTS: Manuelle Gautrand

The showroom for Citroën is inspired by the shape of its products. On street level, the glass façade is minimalist and demonstrates a certain rigor with its flatness and use of large rectangles, but the introduction of the chevron signals the start of a much more original design featuring lozenge shapes. The upper shape is oriented towards the top of the building, and as its three-dimensional character increases with the introduction of prisms, a new depth is brought into to the design. Finally, the top section of the new building is a great glass sculpture that is reminiscent of origami in its complexity. In this exciting project that is midway between a building and a fine art sculpture, the chevron remains present yet discreet, becoming less defined and more suggested in the overall form, and almost subliminal.

06

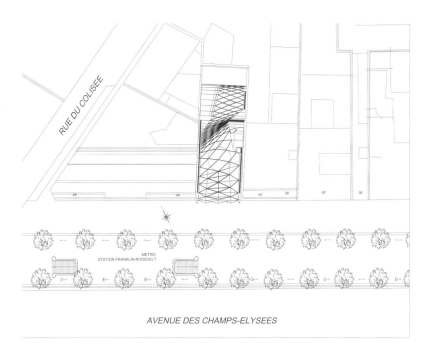

RUE DU COLISEE

METRO
STATION FRANKLIN-ROOSVELT

AVENUE DES CHAMPS-ELYSEES

07

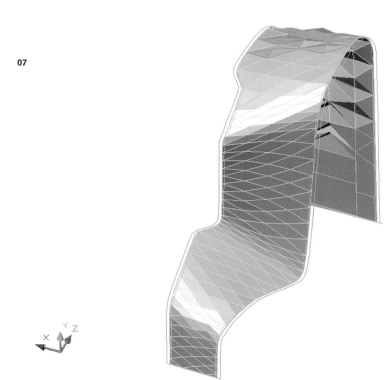

08

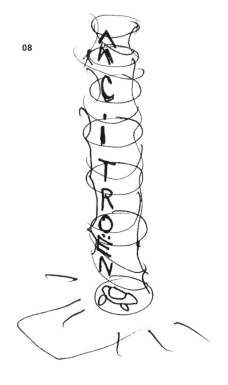

01

ELEVATION A-A SUR PORTE

ELEVATION B-B SUR PORTE

VUE EN PLAN, PORTE

La Lentille Météor Saint-Lazare, 2003
Address: Cour de Rome, Paris, France. **Structural
engineers:** RFR. **Client:** RATP. **Gross floor area:**
8,000 m². **Materials:** doubly-curved glass and stainless
steel structure.

Life in a bubble
ARCHITECTS: Arte Charpentier by Abbès Tahir

For the extension of the fully-automated line to the
St. Lazare station, the Paris Metro Authority (RATP)
planned to build a street-level entrance that would act
as an outstanding symbol of their investment in the
city. The proposal envisioned a glass bubble, "Lentille,"
with a very discreet frame made of stainless steel. This
was achieved by superimposing interlinked arches
onto a double-leaf surface, and by introducing cable
triangulation in the flattened central section. Slender
delta-shaped sections were chosen for the ribs be-
cause of their superior capacity to reflect light. Profiles
are fabricated by extrusion and given a shot-blasted
finish.

01 Elevation and entrance **02** Detail of the arch of door **03** Day view
04 Night view

TECHNICAL

MUSEION – Museum of Modern and Contemporary Art, 2008
Address: Dantestraße 6, Bolzano, Italy. **Project management:** KSV Krüger Schuberth Vandreike, Studio Tecnico, Dr. Ing. Siegfried Pohl. **Structural engineers:** Ingenieurbüro Krone. **Lightning:** Licht Vision. **Client:** Province of Bolzano – South Tyrol. **Gross floor area:** 8,370 m². **Materials:** aluminum, glass, concrete.

Jamb lamp

ARCHITECTS: KSV Krüger Schuberth Vandreike

The effect of the museum building is derived from the contrast between the closed metal skin and the funnel-shaped, transparent entrance façades. These consist of an exterior, point-fixed glass layer and a glazing with inner-thermal properties. Mobile, matt glass lamellas that act to regulate daylight and sun rays are located in the interstitial space between the inner and the outer glass layers. At night, they form a screen for projections; at daytime, they accentuate the access by creating a slanting doorway in the full height of the building. The interstitial space of the façade is used as an active climate layer for creation of an energy efficient buffer.

01 Façade, detail **02** Studios and museum **03** Ground floor plan **04 + 05** Sections **06** Glass façade, entrance

03

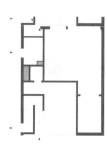

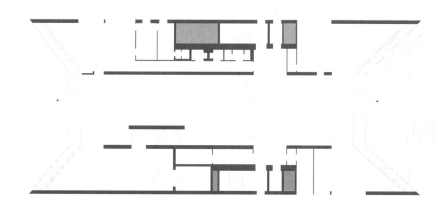

04

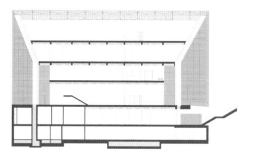

05

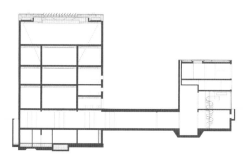

ING Group headquarters, 2002
Address: Amstelveenseweg 500, Amsterdam, The Netherlands. **Client:** Ontwikkelingscombinatie ING Blauwhoed v.o.f. **Gross floor area:** 20,000 m².
Materials: steel, glass double façade skin, concrete.

On high heels

ARCHITECTS: Meyer en Van Schooten

The new ING Group headquarters are built on 12-meter high stilts on a narrow site along the A10 motorway. The building symbolizes the banking and insurance conglomerate as a dynamic, fast-moving international network. Transparency, innovation, eco-friendliness and openness were the key design issues. The glass façade plays an important role in achieving these goals. The double-skin façade allows natural ventilation of the offices without admitting traffic noise. Successive stories intermingle and offer recurrent glimpses. Areas with a panoramic view, like the restaurant, the large conference room and the auditorium, exist alongside introverted spaces. Atriums, loggias, and gardens, both internal and external, are distributed through the building.

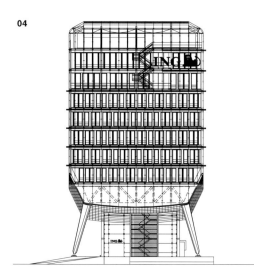

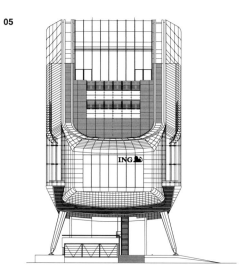

01 South-west façade **02** Double glass façade **03** Interior view double skin **04 + 05** East-west section **06** Longitudinal section **07** Interior view **08** Executive board room

06

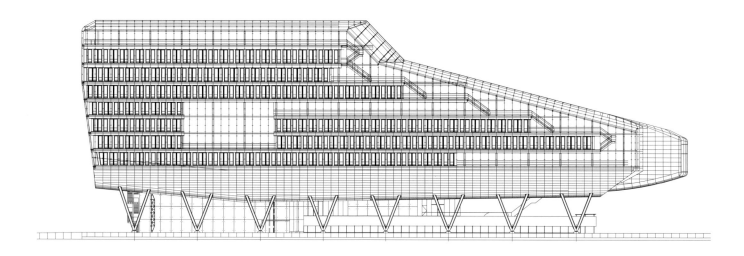

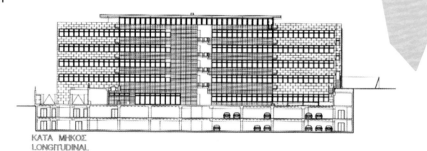

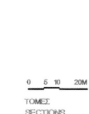

KATA MHKOΣ
LONGITUDINAL

1. ΚΛΕΙΣΤΟ ΑΙΘΡΙΟ -
- ENCLOSED ATRIUM

KATA ΠΛΑΤΟΣ
CROSS

0 5 10   20M

TOMEΣ
SECTIONS

AEGEK S.A. headquarters, 2004
Address: 18-20, Amarousioù, Halandriou street,
Marousi, Athens, Greece. **Client:** AEGEK S.A. General
construction company. **Gross floor area:** 8,000 m²,
respective 12,000 m². **Materials:** metal, glass (okasolar
glazing, laminated triplex).

Under a glass cap
ARCHITECTS: Alexandros N. Tombazis and
associates architects (Meletitiki)

The building is comprised of two long, narrow wings
connected by an enclosed atrium, which supplies am-
ple daylight and natural ventilation. The atrium acts as
an intermediate space between the exterior and interior environment. It is covered by a vaulted glazed roof,
consisting of reflective glass panes and glazing with
incorporated blinds to regulate sunlight and reduce
heating loads. The stack-effect (upward hot air movement) achieved in the atrium contributes to the building's cooling and natural ventilation of the wings. The
two wings are connected via metal bridges with glazed
flooring with an incorporated free-standing staircase.

01 Sections **02** Main stairway with patterned glass threads **03** South-
west wall of atrium

Xicui entertainment center and Zero Energy Media Wall, 2008
Address: 26 Fuxing Road, Haidian District, Beijing, China. **Light planning and façade engineers:** Arup. **Media consultant:** Mark van S., Bernardo Zavattini. **Media content:** Simone Giostra. **Media design:** Jeremy Rotsztain. **Client:** Jingya Corporation. **Gross floor area:** 16,722 m². **Materials:** glass, photovoltaic cells.

Binary windows emulation
ARCHITECTS: Simone Giostra & Partners

The façade of the entertainment center combines one of the largest color LED displays in the world with a photovoltaic system integrated into a glass curtain wall. The building envelope becomes a self-sufficient organic system, harvesting solar energy by day and using it to illuminate the screen after dark, mirroring the day's climatic cycle. The opaque box-like commercial building gains the ability of communicating with its urban environment through a new kind of digital transparency. Its "intelligent skin" interacts with the building interiors and the outer public spaces using embedded, custom-designed software, transforming the building façade into a responsive stage for entertainment and public engagement.

04

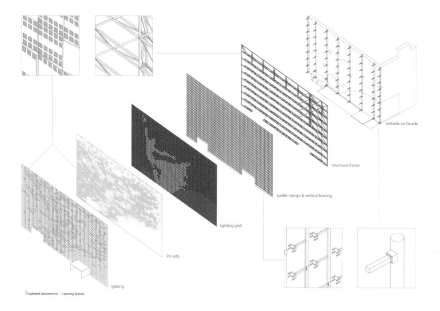

| Exploded Axonometric : Layering System

embeds on facade

structural frame

spider clamps & vertical bracing

lighting grid

PV cells

glazing

05

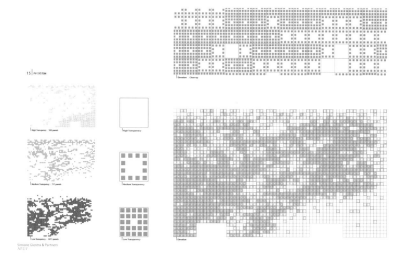

15 | PV SYSTEM

High Transparency : 562 panels

Medium Transparency : 717 panels

Low Transparency : 667 panels

Simone Giostra & Partners
ARUP

High Transparency

Medium Transparency

Low Transparency

Elevation : Close up

Elevation

06

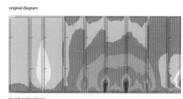

original diagram

traced vector regions

filter / pixelate / color halftone   16pt : default

effect / path / outline stroke / default   170 threshold : 2px blur

ZKM Center for the Arts and Media Technology, 1997
Address: Lorenzstraße 19, Karlsruhe, Germany.
Client: City of Karlsruhe. **Gross floor area:** 38,145 m².
Materials: glass, photovoltaic cells.

Superimposing structures

ARCHITECTS: Architekten Schweger + Partner

ZKM's blue media cube envelopes a hermetically sealed body of the music studios with a light that playfully shines out into the city through the movable glass lamellas. The modular outlines of the photovoltaic system are built in over a 1,000 square meter area of the brick-covered gable roof and cross bars, on the skylights and the newly built cube as well as its façade. The building's concept is the crisscrossing and layering of the inner communication axes and the public intersecting axes of the city. The 100 kilowatt photovoltaic system has another technical feature that goes beyond its integration into a public building: the generator feeds electricity into the city's tram lines using a direct galvanic coupling.

02

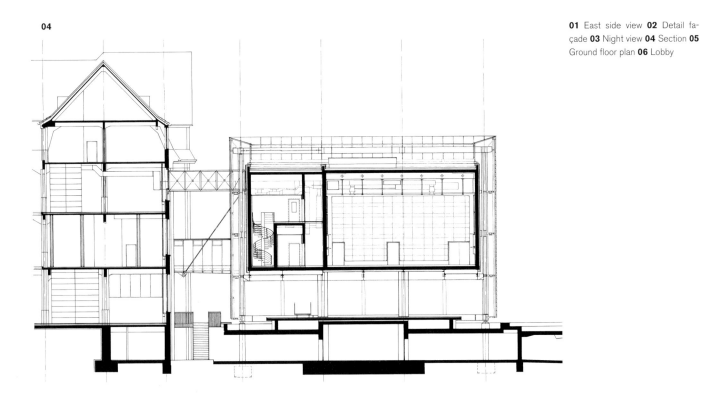

04

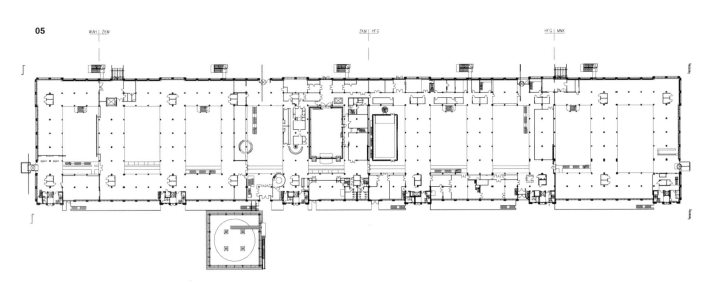

05

01 East side view **02** Detail façade **03** Night view **04** Section **05**
Ground floor plan **06** Lobby

Skywalk Grand Canyon West, 2007
Address: Grand Canyon West, Arizona, USA. **Structural engineers glass basement:** KINON PORZ (Saint-Gobain Deutsche Glas). **Development and production glass breast:** Döring Glas (Saint-Gobain Deutsche Glas). **Client:** Partnership Hualapai native americans, Grand Canyon West/Arizona, with enterpriser David Jin. **Gross floor area:** Glass basement: 147 m². **Materials:** glass, steel.

Like an eagle
ARCHITECTS: MRJ Architects,
Lochsa Engineering, APCO Construction

Grand Canyon, one of the world's most impressive natural wonders, now sports a horseshoe-shaped balcony on one of its banks. The structure rests more than a kilometer above the Colorado River, jutting 21 meters out into the abyss. The floor of the 482-ton steel-and-glass structure consists of 20 square and 26 wedge-shaped compound safety glass elements. The glass floor, sealed with a special laminate, has an area of 147 square meters and can support up to 120 people at a time, amounting to a weight of 750 kilos per square meter. The structure is built to withstand earthquakes reaching 7 on the Richter scale and winds of up to 160 kilometers per hour. A 100-meter long, curved glass railing, made using especially transparent glass panels, completes the illusion of flying over the canyon for those standing on the balcony.

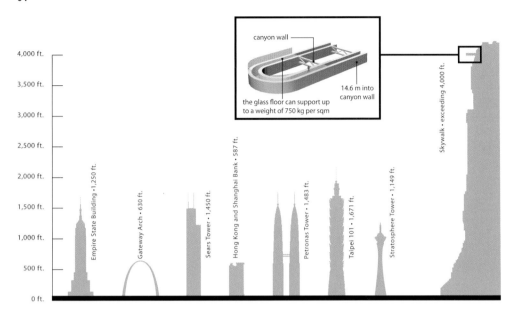

canyon wall

14.6 m into
canyon wall

the glass floor can support up
to a weight of 750 kg per sqm

Skywalk · exceeding 4,000 ft.

4,000 ft.

3,500 ft.

3,000 ft.

2,500 ft.

2,000 ft.

1,500 ft.

1,000 ft.

500 ft.

0 ft.

Empire State Building · 1,250 ft.

Gateway Arch · 630 ft.

Sears Tower · 1,450 ft.

Hong Kong and Shanghai Bank · 587 ft.

Petronas Tower · 1,483 ft.

Taipei 101 · 1,671 ft.

Stratosphere Tower · 1,149 ft.

The Skywalk at Grand Canyon West

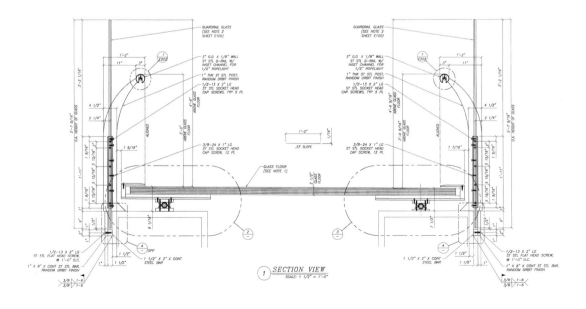

GUARDRAIL GLASS
(SEE NOTE 2
SHEET E100)

3" O.D. X 1/8" WALL
ST STL Q-RAIL W/
INSET CHANNEL FOR
1/2" ROPELIGHT

1" THK ST STL POST,
RANDOM ORBIT FINISH

1/2-13 X 2" LG
ST STL SOCKET HEAD
CAP SCREWS, TYP 5 PL

3/8-24 X 1" LG
ST STL SOCKET HEAD
CAP SCREW, 12 PL

GLASS FLOOR
(SEE NOTE 1)

.33° SLOPE

1'-0"

1/16"

1/2-13 X 2" LG
ST STL FLAT HEAD SCREW,
@ 1'-0" O.C.

1 1/2" X 2" X CONT
STEEL BAR

1" X 8" X CONT ST STL BAR,
RANDOM ORBIT FINISH

① SECTION VIEW
SCALE: 1 1/2" = 1'-0"

6

Glass bridge and walkway over Early Christian mosaics, 2001
Address: Aquileia, Trieste, Italy. **Structural engineers:** Favero & Milan Ingegneria. **Client:** Archdiocese of Gorizia. **Gross floor area:** 282 m². **Materials:** laminated glass, metal.

Over situ

ARCHITECTS: Ottavio Di Blasi & Partners

Every year, more than half a million visitors walk over the floor of Aquileia basilica, slowly but surely wearing away the 4th century mosaics. The glass bridge and floor allow the mosaics to be viewed without being walked on. The new structures cause as little visual impact as possible, and are reversible. The glass walkways in the northern hall, which dates back to the 4th century A. D., are suspended from the ceiling. The glass pathways and footbridge spanning 12.85 meters in the Medieval basilica rest on the column plinths. The pathways and handrails are all made of laminated glass, while the walking surface has been protected from wear and tear by means of a thin removable layer of reinforced glass, protecting the structural glass that is cheap and easy to replace.

04

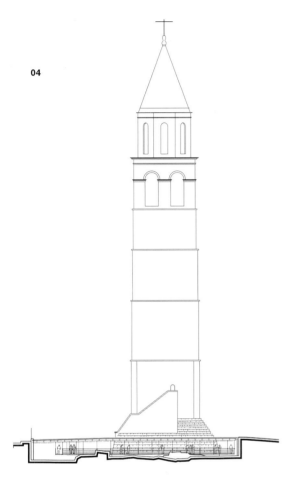

05

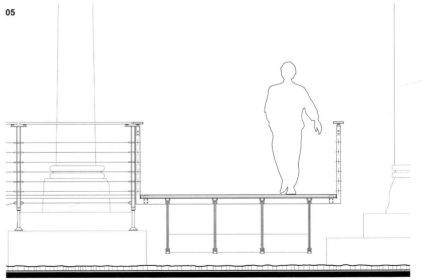

07

Atrium Industry and Chamber of Commerce, 2005
Address: Max-Joseph-Straße 2, Munich, Germany.
Interior design: Ursula Soltmann. **Structural engineers:** Ludwig & Weiler Ingenieure. **Client:** Industry and Chamber of Commerce Munich. **Gross floor area:** 9,500 m². **Materials:** glass.

A new hat
ARCHITECTS: Jutta and Wilhelm Betsch

This project involved the rebuilding and floor plan unification of two listed buildings that were originally used separately and whose independent layouts had been blurred by years of subsequent additions. A new centralized reception and distribution hall with a glazed roof suspended 15 meters from the ground has been turned into a generous spatial center of the entire building. Footbridges connecting the upper stories create the necessary connections between different sections and span the existing height difference. Five composite cantilevers of overlapping glass struts arranged in parallel and affixed using stainless steel clamp elements and inserted bolts are the backbone of the grating. The entire construction corresponds to the structural forces, visualizing the load-baring frame within the largest existing span of a pure glass construction.

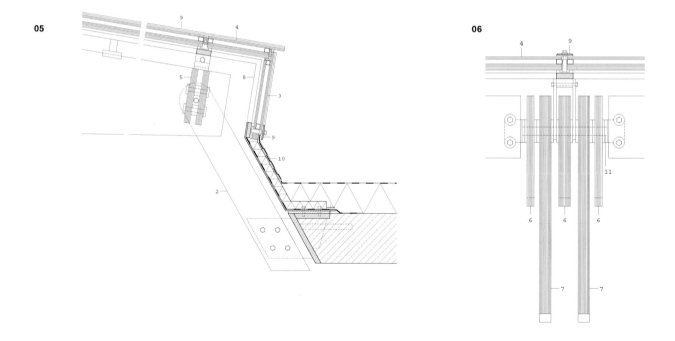

04

05

06

Skywalk, 1998
Address: Münchner Straße, Hanover, Germany. **Structural engineers:** RFR. **Light planning:** Ulrike Brandi Licht. **Client:** Deutsche Messe AG Hannover. **Materials:** steel, glass.

Walk on air

ARCHITECTS: Schulitz + Partner Architekten + Ingenieure

Skywalk was designed and built for the EXPO 2000 as a connecting link between the EXPO train station Laatzen and the EXPO 2000 grounds. The skywalk is an elevated double tube 340 meters in length that runs above Münchner Straße. The double tube simulates the traffic conduit of a tunnel. By minimizing materials of the façade construction, an almost unlimited view of the outside is enabled and the perspective has the effect of increasing the tube's transparency. The completely glazed façade each consists of two curved VSG discs, which are held by linear supports (50 millimeter wide) using point fixations. Simple light tubing above the meshed metal provides night illumination.

04

01 Interior space **02** Entrance
train station Laatzen **03** Night view
04 Bearing structure isometry **05**
Cross section **06** Details façade
07 Inside the tube

05

06

ALLOVER

Berlin main station, 2006
Address: Berlin Hauptbahnhof – Lehrter Bahnhof, Berlin, Germany. **Gross floor area:** 70,000 m².
Materials: glass, concrete, steel.

Crystal clear ICE

ARCHITECTS: gmp – Architekten von Gerkan, Marg und Partner

This historical location is now the intersection of an underground high-speed long distance train track (ICE) with a north-south orientation, and a curved metro and light rail service line 10 meters above ground. The station's structure has been accented using both, urban planning and architectural means, the latter including filigree glass roofs of oversized proportions and two office towers spanning the width of the structure. The 430-meter long departure hall is covered by an impressive, intricate glass roof, sectioned to indicate the above-ground, as well as the north-south below-ground platforms. The volume as a whole acts as an inviting gateway to the government quarter and the Moabit area, bordering to the north. The arching light rail bridges were constructed using a support-free steel construction, curved in three directions.

01 + 02 Glass façade detail **03** Interior view **04** Site plan **05** Sketch **06** Section **07** Façade

04

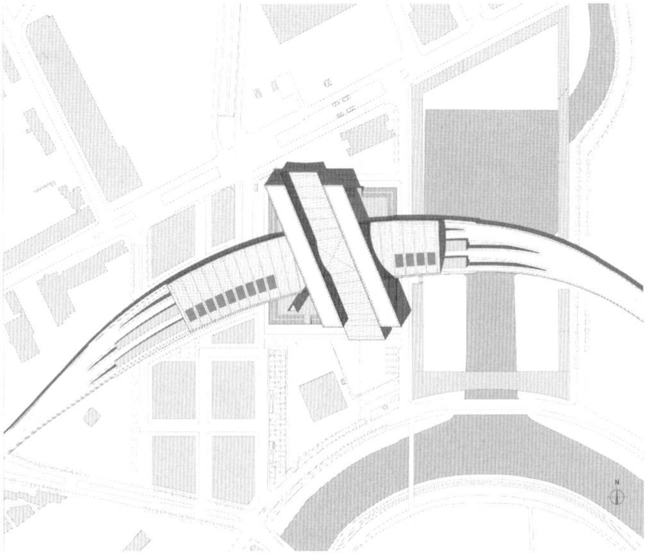

05

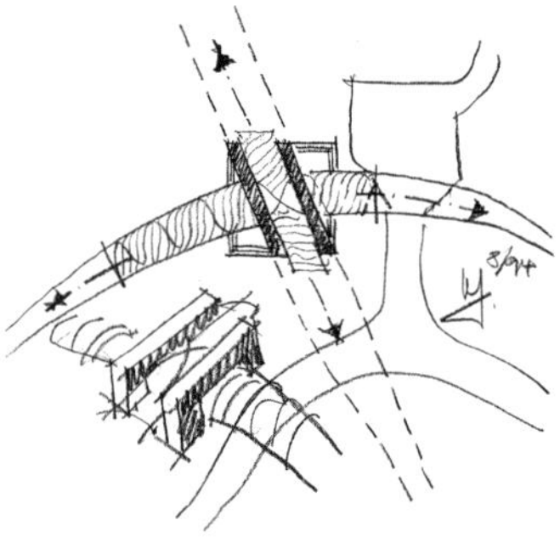

06

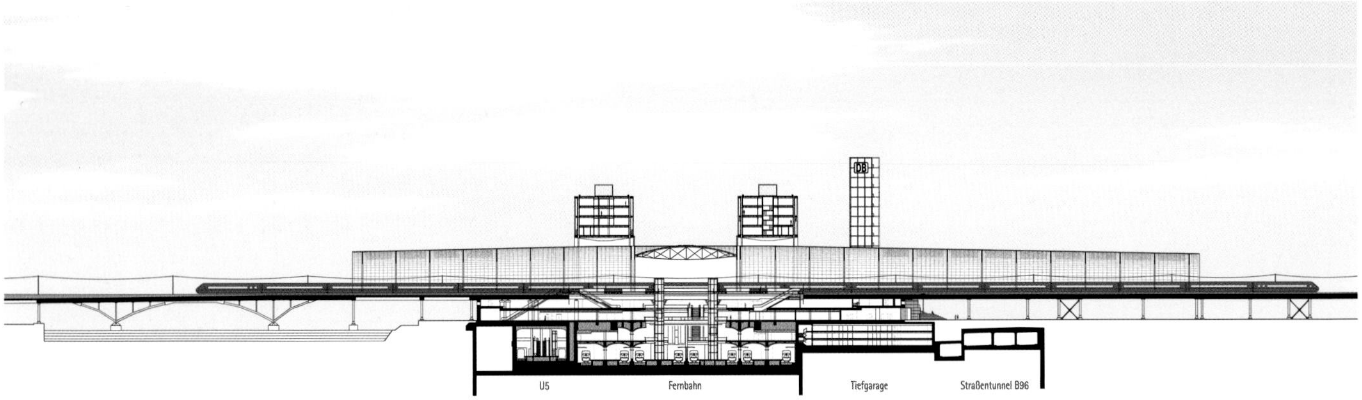
DB
U5
Fernbahn
Tiefgarage
Straßentunnel B96

01

Victoria ensemble, 1997
Address: Sachsenring 81–85, Cologne, Germany.
Client: Victoria Lebensversicherung AG. **Gross floor area:** 25,000 m². **Materials:** anti-sun glass, aluminum, nero assoluto, Iragna gneis.

Constructivist composition

ARCHITECTS: Thomas van den Valentyn and
Armin Tillmann / van den Valentyn – Architektur

The project consist of three parts: the double towers with glass façade, a glass building with an atrium and a linear black stone building, referring to the black building by Egon Eiermann next to it and a significantly lower vocational school designed by Hans Schilling. The cylinders narrow slightly on their way up, contrasted by the main volume's cube which gains in dimensions in its upper section. The form of the double circular building is a reference to the Russian constructivist Konstantin Melnikov, whose tower pair went up in Moscow in 1927. Both cylinders, melting one into the other, are slightly tilted and stand in front of the glazed cube, underlining their independence from the main volume. The main building's glass façade winds around a generous, strictly geometrical glass-covered atrium. It has conical double glass façade.

02

04

Rinhhahn ← Victoria → Eismn

05

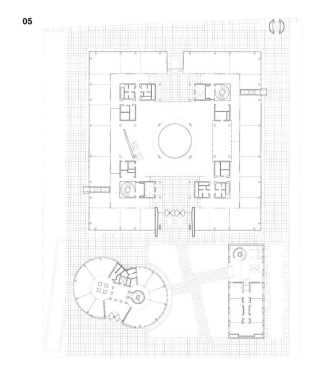

06

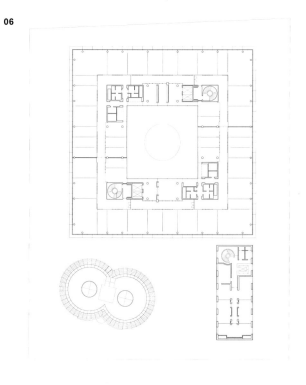

210

01

Herz Jesu church, 2000
Address: Lachner Straße 8, Munich, Germany. **Artists:**
A. Beleschenko, Lutzenberger & Lutzenberger, M+M,
M. Wähner, A. Leonie. **Client:** Archdiocese of Munich.
Gross floor area: 1,450 m². **Materials:** steel, glass,
wood, reinforced concrete, natural stone, red brass
canvas.

Knockin' on heaven's door

ARCHITECTS: Allmann Sattler Wappner
Architekten

The church is an open building that is full of light and
life. The transition from the church square though the
atrium and into the inner space is smooth and can be
adjusted if needed. The glass façade wraps around
an inner membrane of maple lamellas. Due to the
different materiality of these two nested cubes, light
of changing colors and intensity reaches inside the
church. The arrangement of the vertical wooden lamellas creates lighting that continuously increases
in brightness in the direction of the altar, simultaneously protecting this area from being visible from
the outside through the opaque façade. The front of
the building consists of an intensely blue glass gate
stretching along the building's full height, and which is
used on high holydays.

212

02

04

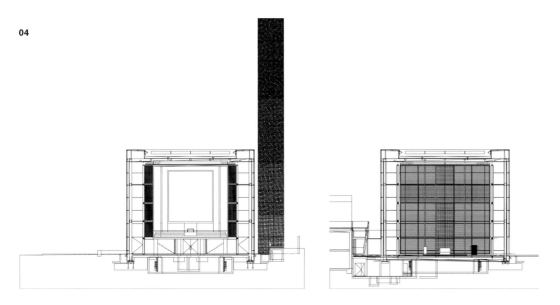

05

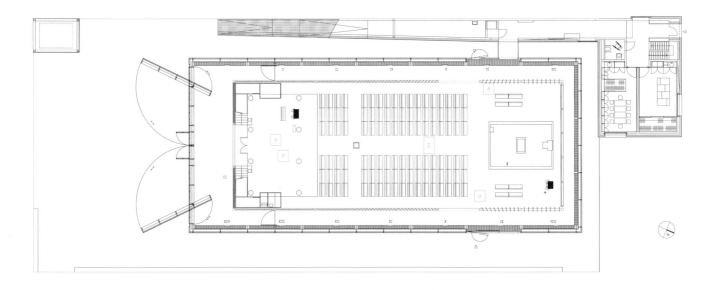

Mercedes Welt am Salzufer, 2000
Address: Salzufer 1, Berlin, Germany. **Project management:** DaimlerChrysler Bauabteilung. **Client:** DaimlerChrysler AG Stuttgart. **Gross floor area:** 35,500m². **Materials:** glass, steel.

The Ship-inn
ARCHITECTS: Lamm - Weber - Donath

The sculptural architecture of the 22-meter high, six-story steel frame construction with a glass façade follows the shape of the bank of the Landwehrkanal and its curved roof is reminiscent of a ship's hull. A 750-year old olive tree imported from Italy stands at the center of the ground floor, the so-called market, and is surrounded by a restaurant. Additional attractions include a 40 square meter video screen, two indoor climbing walls next to a waterfall, a Formula 1 race simulator and a children's street traffic school. The concept follows the principle of New York's Guggenheim Museum in that the individual levels are connected by flat, sloping exhibition ramps. Glass paneling above the second floor bears a transparent point-pattern which allows unhindered views while helping control incoming sunlight.

216

04

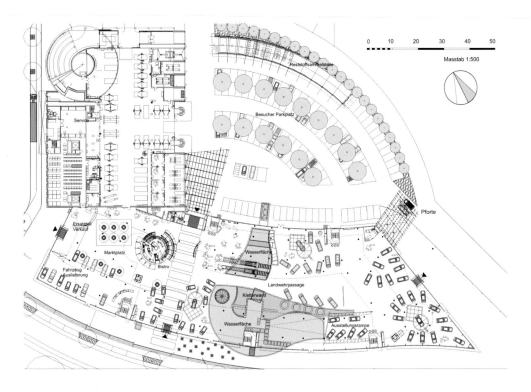

01 Façade in the early morning light **02** Atrium **03** View in the early morning light **04** First floor plan **05** Sections **06** South-east pike "bow" **07** Pike inside with conference room

Masstab 1:500

05

07

01

Treetop apartments, 2002
Address: Herthastraße 18, Hanover Kirchrode, Germany. **Glass engineers:** Burmester + Sellmann. **Client:** Jürgen Erdmann. **Gross floor area:** 1,130 m². **Materials:** steel, glass covering wood.

Men in trees

ARCHITECTS: Despang Architekten

The residential and commercial building is an urban equivalent of living in a treetop. It achieves this by imitating the airy and light-filled setting found between the braches by alternating wood and glass and opening itself up to the existing street greenery and the sun. The wooden balcony boxes act to create acoustic privacy from the neighbors and gather the maximum amount of light. Glass layers in front of wood facing create an energo-thermal buffer and simultaneously protect the material from the effects of weathering and vandalism. The building is dematerialized by its glass envelope and thanks to its reflective properties becomes a part of the neighborhood and the urban greenery.

02

04

0 1 2 3 4 5m

05

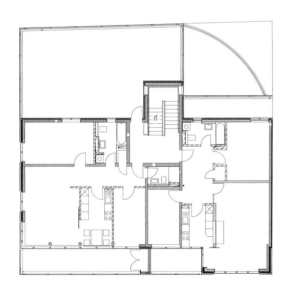

06

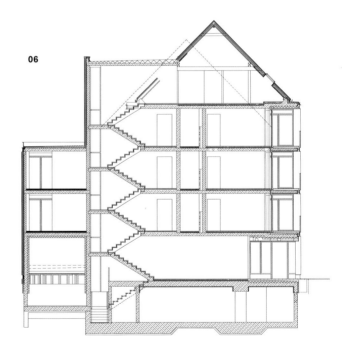

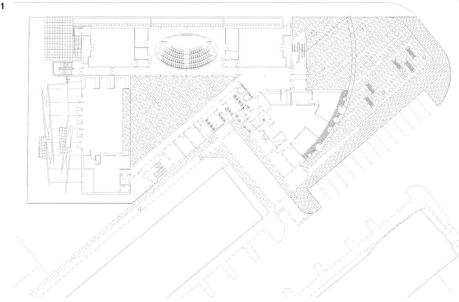

08

01

Wolfson Medical School Building, 2002
Address: University of Glasgow, University Avenue, Glasgow, United Kingdom. **Quantity surveyor:** Turner & Townsend. **Structural engineers:** URS Corporation. **Mechanical and electrical engineers:** Hulley & Kirkwood. **Lighting designer:** Gavin Fraser. **Landscape architect:** Gross Max. **Contractor:** Costain Group PLC. **Client:** University of Glasgow. **Materials:** three story curved glass double skin wall, all-glass roof, stone and render.

Glassical modernism
ARCHITECTS: Reiach and Hall Architects

The three articulated blocks arranged around a triangular atrium with a fully glazed roof were built in response to a very specific user brief and to the inner city's master plan strategy (also developed by Reiach and Hall). Built with a succinct purpose, the project provides an innovative learning environment for medical undergraduates with facilities to support a problem-based learning curriculum. The New Medical School Building accommodates a dean's suite, a curved three-story all-glass double-skinned open plan study landscape, lecture theaters, break-out spaces, an atrium court, which has become the social heart of the school, mock hospital ward, seminar rooms, assembly spaces, catering facility, office accommodation and underground parking.

01 Ground floor plan **02** Exterior view **03** Atrium **04** Night view

02

Terrence Donnelly Centre for Cellular and Molecular Biology Research, 2005
Address: 150 College Street, Toronto, Canada. **Structural engineers:** Yolles Partnership and Knippers & Helbig; H. H. Angus & Associates. **Client:** University of Toronto. **Gross floor area:** 20,750 m². **Materials:** steel, concrete, glass.

Lucent research

ARCHITECTS: Behnisch Architekten with architectsAlliance

University of Toronto is a leading institution for medical research. The new research and laboratory building, a 12-story transparent cube, corresponds to the university's interdisciplinary concept. The lower building section is designed as a nuanced architectural landscape and is publicly accessible. It houses offices, seminar rooms and a cafeteria. Laboratories and other work rooms on the upper floors are laid out in a highly flexible fashion. By forgoing the use of suspended ceilings and therefore leaving the plumbing and load-bearing structures open, as well as by using simple and durable materials, a light, loft-like atmosphere is created. In addition, the relatively narrow floor layout allows excellent use of natural daylight. Two and three-storied lounges enhance the work atmosphere with recreation areas and improvised work spaces.

04

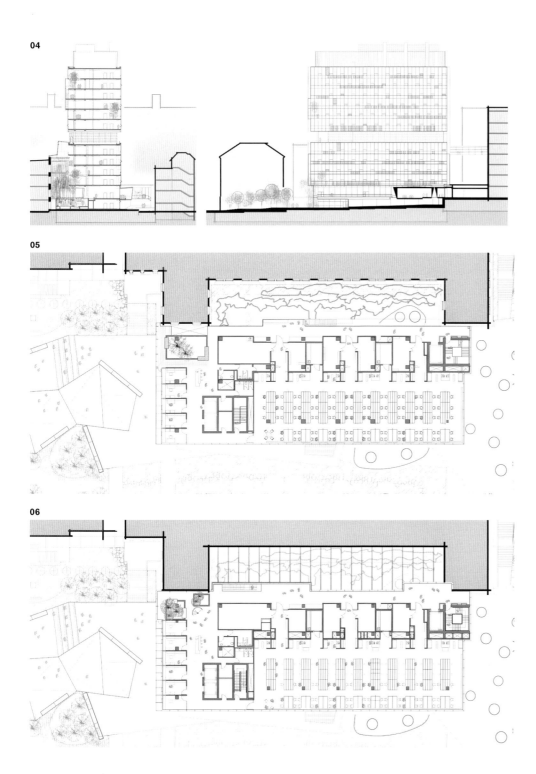

05

06

01 View from east Queens Park
02 East façade 03 South façade
with main entrance 04 Section 05
Second floor plan 06 Eleventh floor
plan 07 Public thoroughfare on the
first floor 08 Garden on the third
floor

Beatson Institute Cancer Research, 2007
Address: Garscube Estate, Switchback Road, Bearsden, Glasgow, United Kingdom. **Quantity surveyor:** Turner & Townsend. **Structural engineers:** URS Corporation. **Services engineers:** Hulley & Kirkwood Consulting Engineers. **Landscape architects:** Ian White Associates. **Contractor:** Balfour Beatty Construction Ltd. **Artist:** Alan Johnston. **Client:** University of Glasgow and Cancer Research UK. **Materials:** crystalline cube of glass and steel.

Shelter behind gossamer walls

ARCHITECTS: Reiach and Hall Architects

This major research laboratory building accommodates a directorate, seminar rooms, lecture theater, social areas and laboratories with support spaces for a staff of 250. It is located on the premises of the walled-in garden grounds of the University of Glasgow's existing Garscube Estate research campus. The new building takes the form of a horizontally layered crystalline glazed cube. The ground floor, containing lecture, meeting and café areas, opens up to the enclosed garden. Above, a series of highly serviced laboratories encircle a central communal area. A solar screen grid was 'drawn' onto the glazed walls of the exterior. This cutting-edge, glazed skin building is seen as a world leader in part due to its excellent open debate, forum and research environment.

01 Lecture theater **02** Exterior
detail **03** General view **04** Sketch
05 Site plan and entry level plan
06 Section **07** Crystalline cube

04

05

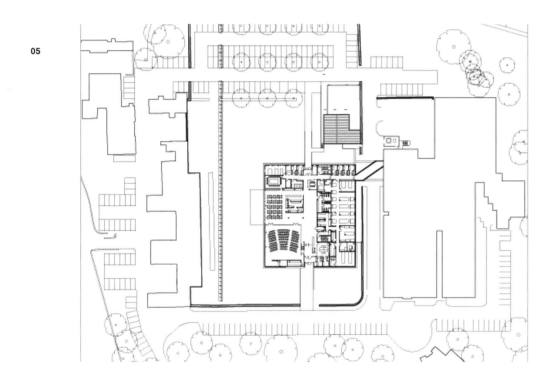

06

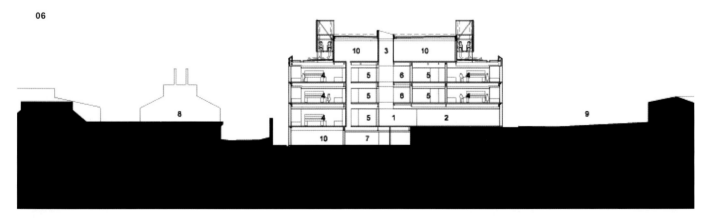

Adidas employee restaurant "Stripes", 1999
Address: Adi-Dassler-Straße 1–2, Herzogenaurach,
Germany. **Project management:** Stefan Däfler. **Project
architect:** Andreas Grabow. **Structural engineers:**
Pfefferkorn Ingenieure. **Energy engineers:** Transsolar.
Landscape architects: GTL Landschaftsarchitekten.
Client: adidas-Salomon AG. **Gross floor area:** 2,020 m².
Materials: Façade: insulating glass in steel frame,
wood. Roof: printed glass.

It's picnic time
ARCHITECTS: Kauffmann Theilig & Partner

The new restaurant is located in a forest clearing, and
is oriented toward a neighboring lake. Eating in the
middle of the woods is the recurring motif of the building. Multiple terraces integrated into the slightly sloping plot structure the various atmospheric areas inside
and outside of the building. A glass envelope surrounds
the area and defines the interior space, the restaurant.
The construction rests on irregularly arranged, scaled
stilts which reproduce the image of tree trunks in the
forest. A glass roof, completed as a double-leaf structure with an internally-lying rear-ventilated special film
which serves climate, acoustic and sunlight regulation
roles, rests on the stilts. All service functions are hidden
inside the slope.

03

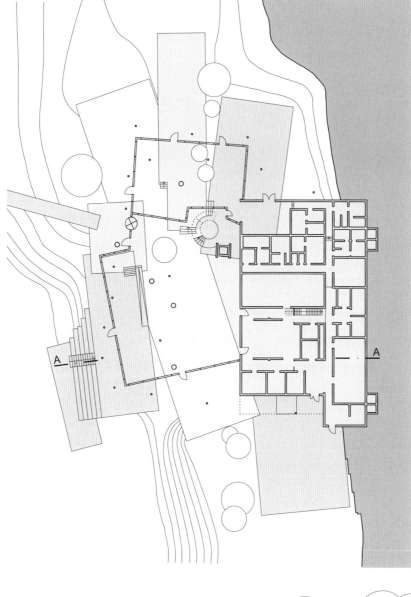

04

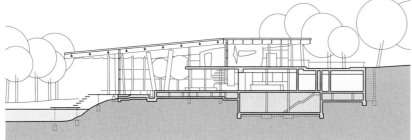

Prospect Park condominium, 2009
Address: One Grand Army Plaza, Brooklyn, NY, USA.
Architect of record: Stephen B. Jacobs Group PC.
Developers: Seventeen Development, LLC. **Sales agent:**
Corcoran Group Marketing. **Client:** Seventeen Development, LLC. **Gross floor area:** 22,297 m². **Materials:**
concrete, aluminum, glass, hardwood, granite.

On the bright side of life

ARCHITECTS: Richard Meier & Partners
Architects

Located on a prominent corner of Prospect Park in Brooklyn, the architecture is intended to enhance the urban space of Grand Army Plaza while establishing new relationships to the main arteries and the historic context. The base of the building respects the existing scale and diversity of the immediate context and completes the city block, while the tower lends landmark status to the building within the overall urban setting. The building's striking sculpted glass form promotes maximum transparency while reflecting the variety of the surrounding context. Natural sunlight animates the building, lending vitality to the surrounding streetscape, landscape, and community. Virtually all apartments have balconies with spectacular views in various directions.

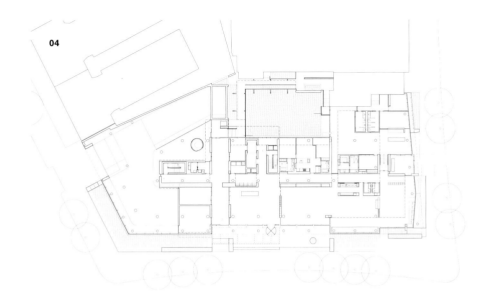

04

01 Exterior detail **02** Bathroom panoramic **03** Exterior (looking northeast from Grand Army Plaza) **04** Ground floor plan **05** Eighth floor plan **06** Site plan **07** Exterior (looking south toward Prospect Park) **08** Night view

05

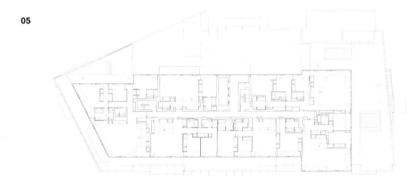

06

Eawag Forum, 2006
Address: Überlandstrasse 133, Dübendorf, Switzerland. **Client:** Eawag, the Swiss Federal Institute of Aquatic Science and Technology. **Gross floor area:** 8,533 m². **Materials:** screenprinted, position of the sun controlled glass gills in front of a Eternit-façade, glass spandrels in the atrium.

Radiator ribs

ARCHITECTS: Bob Gysin + Partner BGP

The expressive outer layer of the façade consisting of glass lamellas is the building's calling card. The screen-printed glass lamellas track the position of the sun, functioning as sun protection in the summer and as passive sun energy collectors in the winter. The thermal layer found below consists of structural glass alternating with highly warmth insulating wood elements. The spaces suited for various uses have a U-shaped layout around a five story-high atrium, which is transformed into a true spatial experience thanks to its meeting boxes, stairs and interesting visual relationships. Communication zones, seminar rooms, lecture halls, a library as well as a restaurant complete the variegated space and create an attractive work atmosphere.

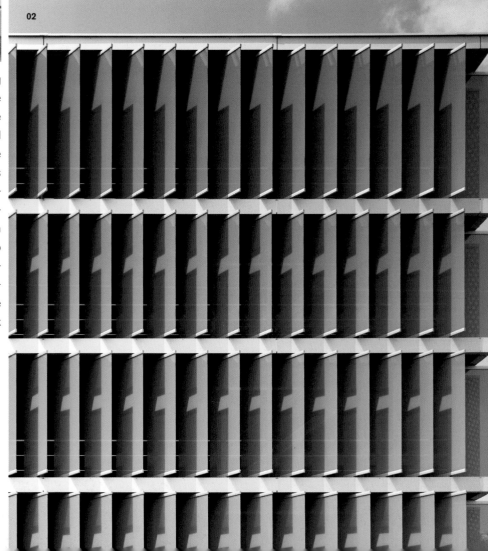

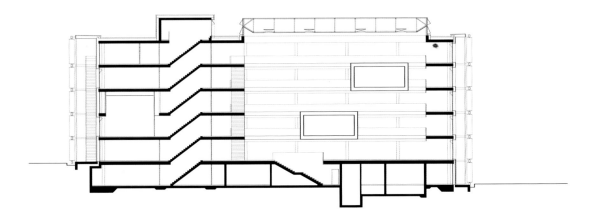

05

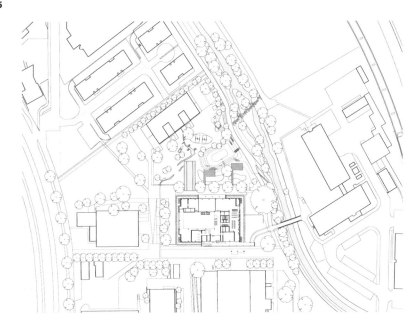

ADVA AG Optical Networking, 2006
Address: Märzenquelle 1–3, Meiningen, Germany.
Project management: Armin Fiess, Marco Ossmann.
Project architects: Ralf Pfeiffer, Christian Übele,
Ralf Müller. **Light concept:** Transsolar. **Structural
engineers:** Pfefferkorn Ingenieure. **Client:** ADVA AG
Optical Networking. **Gross floor area:** 5,950 m².
Materials: double glazing, wood, steel.

Now I begin to see

ARCHITECTS: Kauffmann Theilig & Partner

The ADVA AG Optical Networking company develops
and manufactures fiber optical products. The two-story
building is an expression of the new company's phi-
losophy and stance: transparency, communication and
desirable, light-filled workplaces for each employee.
Glass separating walls allow concentration, and simultaneously encourage cooperation. Roof elements with
integrated light wells lead daylight to every desk. This
principle is continued using courtyards located in the
newly built areas. The building's structure is modular
and highly flexible: wooden façade elements on the
northern and southern sides are delimiters for additional building sections.

04

05

06

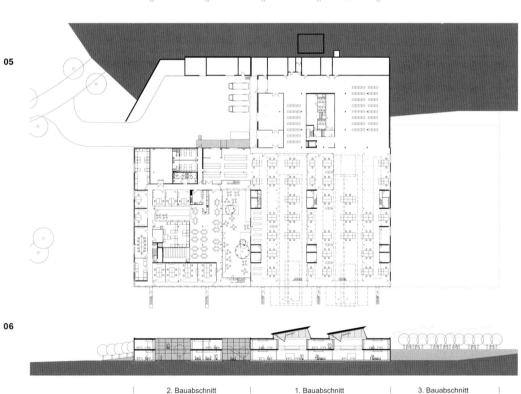

| 2. Bauabschnitt | 1. Bauabschnitt | 3. Bauabschnitt |

RCHITECTS

Index

**DOK architecten
(Liesbeth van der Pol)** → 14
Entrepotdok 86
1001 ME Amsterdam
(The Netherlands)
T +31.20.3449700
F +31.20.3449799
post@dokarchitecten.nl
www.dokarchitecten.nl

E

Emergent → 52
2404 Wilshire Boulevard, Suite 8D
Los Angeles, CA 90057 (USA)
T +1.213.3851475
contact@emergentarchitecture.com
www.emergentarchitecture.com

F

Fontana und Partner → 24
Via Nova 14
7017 Flims Dorf (Switzerland)
T +41.81.9209640
F +41.81.9209649
info@fontana-und-partner.ch
www.fontana-und-partner.ch

Foster + Partners → 78
Riverside Three, 22 Hester Road
London SW11 4AN (United Kingdom)
T +44.20.77380455
F +44.20.77381107
press@fosterandpartners.com
www.fosterandpartners.com

G

GATERMANN + SCHOSSIG → 62
Richartzstraße 10
50667 Cologne (Germany)
T +49.221.9258210
F +49.221.92582170
info@gatermann-schossig.de
www.gatermann-schossig.de

Manuelle Gautrand → 160
39, boulevard de la Bastille
75012 Paris (France)
T +33.1.56950646
F +33.1.56950647
contact@manuelle-gautrand.com
www.manuelle-gautrand.com

**Simone Giostra & Partners
Architects** → 178
55 Washington Street, Suite 454
New York City, NY 11201 (USA)
T +1.212.9208180
F +1.212.9208180
info@sgp-architects.com
www.sgp-architects.com

**gmp – Architekten von Gerkan,
Marg und Partner** → 204
Elbchaussee 139
22763 Hamburg (Germany)
T +49.40.881510
F +49.40.88151177
hamburg-e@gmp-architekten.de
www.gmp-architekten.de

Gottlieb Paludan Architects A/S
→ 144
Finsensvej 6e
2000 Frederiksberg (Denmark)
T +45.3814.4545
F +45.3814.4555
gp@gottliebpaludan.com
www.gottliebpaludan.com

Guedes Cruz Architects → 136
Rua Monte Olivete 53
1200-279 Lisbon (Portugal)
T +351.21.3967245
F +351.21.3977938
atelier@guedescruz.com
www.guedescruz.com

GWJARCHITEKTEN Bern → 28
Nordring 4A
3000 Berne 25 (Switzerland)
T +41.31.3408222
F +41.31.3408200
mailbox@gwj.ch
www.gwj.ch

H

**Theo Hotz AG Architekten +
Planer** → 42, 82
Münchaldenstrasse 21, Postfach
8034 Zurich (Switzerland)
T +41.44.4224733
F +41.44.4225711
info@theohotz.ch
www.theohotz.ch

I

**Jean Marc Ibos Myrto Vitart
architects** → 152
4 Cité Paradis
75010 Paris (France)
T +33.1.44838580
F +33.1.44838581
jmimv@ibosvitart.com
www.ibosvitart.com

J

**Jensen & Skodvin Arkitekt-
kontor AS** → 18
Fredensborgveien 11
0177 Oslo (Norway)
T +47.22.994899
F +47.22.994888
office@jsa.no
www.jsa.no

JHK Architecten → 36
Postbus 3328
3502 GH Utrecht
(The Netherlands)
T +31.30.2964060
F +31.30.2913436
info@jhk.nl
www.jhk.nl

K

Kauffmann Theilig & Partner,
Freie Architekten BDA
→ 234, 246
Zeppelinstraße 10
73760 Ostfildern (Germany)
T +49.711.451220
F +49.711.4512240
info@ktp-architekten.de
www.ktp-architekten.de

Klein Dytham architecture
→ 96
AD Building 2F
1-15-7 Hiroo, Shibuya-ku
Tokyo 150-0012 (Japan)
T +81.3.57952277
F +81.3.57952276
kda@klein-dytham.com
www.klein-dytham.com

KSV Krüger Schuberth
Vandreike → 168
Brunnenstraße 196
10119 Berlin (Germany)
T +49.30.2830310
F +49.30.28303110
ksv@ksv-network.de
www.ksv-network.de

L

Lamm - Weber - Donath
GmbH → 216
Bockelstraße 146
70619 Stuttgart (Germany)
T +49.711.449920
F +49.711.4499299
lwd@lwd-architekten.de
www.lwd-architekten.de

Lochsa Engineering → 186
6345 South Jones Blvd., Suite 100
Las Vegas, NV 89118 (USA)
T +1.702.3659312
F +1.702.3659317
resume@lochsa.com
www.lochsa.com

M

Maki and Associates → 40
13–4 Hachiyama-cho Shibuya-ku
Tokyo 150-0035 (Japan)
T +81.3.37803880
F +81.3.37803881
fmaki@maki-and-associates.co.jp
www.maki-and-associates.co.jp

Mecanoo architecten → 50
Oude Delft 203
2601 DG Delft (The Netherlands)
T +31.15.2798100
F +31.15.2798111
info@mecanoo.nl
www.mecanoo.nl

Alexandros M. Tombazis and associates
architects Meletitiki Ltd. → 176
27, Monemvasias Street
151 25 Polydroso – Athens (Greece)
T +30.210.6800690
F +30.210.6801005
meletitiki@hol.gr
www.meletitiki.gr

Meyer en Van Schooten Architecten
→ 102, 172
Pilotenstraat 35
1059 CH Amsterdam (The Netherlands)
T +31.20.5319800
F +31.20.5319801
office@mvsa.nl
www.mvsa.nl

MRJ Architects → 186
4790 W. University Ave.
Las Vegas, NV 89103 (USA)
T +1.702.8693808
F +1.702.8693813
info@mrjarchitects.com
www.mrjarchitects.com
www.destinationgrandcanyon.com

Murphy / Jahn
→ 32, 90
35 East Wacker Drive, 3rd Floor
Chicago, IL 60601 (USA)
T +1.312.4277300
F +1.312.3320274
info@murphyjahn.com
www.murphyjahn.com

N

nps tchoban voss GbR Architekten BDA
Alf M. Prasch Sergei Tchoban Ekkehard Voss
→ 120, 156
Rosenthaler Straße 40/41
10178 Berlin (Germany)
T +49.30.2839200
F +49.30.283920200
berlin@npstv.de
www.npstv.de

O

ORMS Architecture Design → 58
1 Pine street
London, EC1R 0JH (United Kingdom)
T +44.20.78338533
orms@orms.co.uk
www.orms.co.uk

P

Periphériques architectes
→ 100
T +33.1.44920501
agence@peripheriques-architectes.com
www.peripheriques-architectes.com

Picture Credits

Alpbach Tourismus GmbH 69 b.
Arban, Tom 226, 227, 229
Archigraphie, Steffen Vogt, Stuttgart
54 r., 55, 57
Atelier 106, Berlin 168 (portrait)
Bartelsman, Jan 17
Baumann, Olaf, Hanover
20, 21, 23, 220, 221, 223
Betsch, Jutta and Wilhelm 194–197
Boegly, Luc 100, 101
Boy de la Tour, Didier 164 b., 165
Bredt, Marcus 204 r., 205, 207
Breukel, Koos, Amsterdam
102 (portrait), 172 (portrait)
Bucher, Alain, Berne 28 r., 29, 31
Burmester, Christian 54 (portrait)
Cano, Enrico, Como 46 b., 47, 49
Cecil, Mathieu 160 (portrait)
Cook, Peter / View 58, 59, 61
Daici, Ano, Tokyo 96, 97, 99
Daniilides, N. 6/7, 176 r. b., 177
Danuser, Gaudenz, Flims 24–26
Despang Architekten 128–131
Eggimann, Marc © MCH Messe
Schweiz AG Basel 42 r., 43, 44 r. a., 44 r. b.
Engelhardt / Sellin 90 a., 91
Esch, H. G. 90 b.
Fessy, George, Lyon
152 r., 153, 155, 172 r., 173, 175
Gatermann + Schossig 62, 65 r.
Grand Canyon West 186, 187, 188 b., 189 l.
Ferrero, Alberto 118, 119
Flittner, Bettina 62 (portrait l.)
Fraser, Gavin 225
Frei, Roger, Zurich 242, 243, 245
Simone Giostra & Partners 178–181
Guerra, Fernado 136, 137, 139
Halbe, Roland, Architekturfotografie
234, 235, 237, 246, 247, 249
van der Hoek, Allard, Amsterdam
102, 105
Holzherr, Florian, Munich 212 r., 213, 215
Hunter, Keith 224 b.
Hursley, Tim 148, 149, 151
Jensen & Skodvin Architects 18, 19
Jungfer, Julia, Berlin 120–122

Kandzia, Christian 70 a.
Kawara, Tom © Theo Hotz AG Zurich
42 (portrait), 82 (portrait)
KINON Porz/Grand Canyon West 188 a.
Kitajima, Toshiharu 41
Knauf, Holger / Anin • Jeromin •
Fitilidis & Partner 140, 141, 143
Kokkalias, N. 176 (portrait)
Kramer, Luuk, Amsterdam 103
Kroll, Bernhard 182 r., 183, 185
Laignel, Eric © LWD / Stuttgart
216 b., 219
Linden, John 93
Lindhe, Jens 144 b., 145
Lindman, Åke E:son 10, 11, 13
Mader, Rainer, Cologne 208, 209, 211
Maki and Associates 40 b.
Martig, Caspar, Berne 28 (portrait)
Richard Meier & Partners Architects
LLP / dbox 238 r., 239, 241
Meuser, Philipp 156 (portrait)
Müller, Stefan, Berlin 114 r., 115, 117
Musi, Pino, Milan 46 a.
Narodizkij, Alekseij 157, 159
nps tchoban voss, Berlin 156 r.
Ouwerkerk, Erik-Jan 182 (portrait)
Palladium Photodesign, Cologne
36, 37, 39
Pfändler, Beat, Zurich 46 (portrait)
Pyykkö, Matti 77
QWA 86, 87, 89
Richters, Christian, Münster 50, 51
Riller, René, Schlanders 168 r., 169
Riolzi, Paolo, Milan 171
Rose, Corinne, Berlin 114 (portrait)
Ruault, Philippe 160 r., 161, 162
Ryberg, Bent 144 a., 147
Saint-Gobain Exprover 189 r.
Schiblon, Andreas, Medienzentrum
Rheinland 65 l.
Schmitz, Arjen 14, 15
Schodder, Martin 70 b., 71, 73
Schroeder, Richard 152 (portrait)
Schulitz + Partner, Brunswick 198–201
Seggelke, Ute Karen 204 (portrait)
Seliger, Mark 238 (portrait)
Doug Snower Photography 32, 33, 35

Theo Hotz AG Zurich 44 l.
Tiainen, Jussi 74, 75
Topuntoli, Stefano 190, 191, 193
Unterhauser, Josefine, Riedering
110, 111, 113
Walti, Ruedi, Basel 106, 107, 109
Weishaupt Max GmbH Schwendi DE
82, 83, 85
Weiss, Klaus-Dieter 63
Wesener, Wolfgang, Cavaso del Tomba
212 (portrait)
Wett, Günter Richard, Innsbruck
66, 67, 69 a.
Winkel © Mercedes-Benz / Berlin
216 a., 217
Wintermans, Paul 86 (portrait)
Yoshida, Makoto
124, 125, 127, 132, 133, 135,
Young, Nigel / Foster + Partners
78, 79, 81
Zanre, Paul 230, 231, 233

All other pictures, especially the portraits and plans not mentioned above, were made available by the architects.

Cover

front side: Holger Knauf / Anin • Jeromin •
Fitilidis & Partner
back side: Marcus Bredt (l.)
Nigel Young / Foster + Partners (r.)